Selenium 1.0 Testing Tools

Beginner's Guide

Test your web applications with multiple browsers using the Selenium Framework to ensure the quality of web applications

David Burns

BIRMINGHAM - MUMBAI

Selenium 1.0 Testing Tools

Beginner's Guide

First published: November 2010

Production Reference: 1171110

Published by Packt Publishing Ltd.
32 Lincoln Road
Olton
Birmingham, B27 6PA, UK.

ISBN 978-1-849510-26-4

www.packtpub.com

Cover Image by Duraid Fatouhi (duraidfatouhi@yahoo.com)

Credits

Author
David Burns

Reviewers
Tarun Kumar Bhadauria
Sameer Borate

Acquisition Editor
Usha Iyer

Development Editors
Neha Mallik
Rakesh Shejwal

Technical Editor
Aaron Rosario

Copy Editor
Lakshmi Menon

Indexer
Tejal Daruwale

Editorial Team Leader
Aanchal Kumar

Project Team Leader
Priya Mukherji

Project Coordinator
Zainab Bagasrawala

Proofreader
Mario Cecere

Graphics
Nilesh Mohite
Geetanjali Sawant

Production Coordinator
Melwyn D'sa

Cover Work
Melwyn D'sa

About the Author

David Burns is a Senior Developer in Test having worked with Selenium for quite a few years. David is a Selenium Core Committer, so he knows and understands what users and developers want from the framework.

I would like to thank my wife for supporting me while I was writing my book and making sure I did things on time.

I would also like to thank the other Selenium Committers for answering my questions and cheering me on to finish the book.

About the Reviewers

Tarun Kumar Bhadauria is an Electronics Engineer and hails from Gwalior. He has been involved with software testing for over five years. He spent most of his career with QA practices for the Indian division of CIBER. He is currently associated with Tavant Technologies Bangalore. He has worked on a gamut of testing fields that encompasses Manual Testing, Performance Testing and Functional Test Automation using both commercial and open source tools. His primary inclination has been towards functional test automation using Selenium.

Tarun has been key contributor to Official Selenium Documentation and was recognized as co-author for Selenium documentation release 1.0 by Selenium Head Quarters.

His spare moments are spent in exercise and blogging.

Sameer Borate is an independent web developer based in Pune, India. He has been developing web applications using PHP and MySQL since 2000, when PHP was just a blip on the web radar, and now spends most of his time working with XHTML, PHP, XML, MySQL, and JavaScript. For the last few years he has been helping small companies design web application architectures for their clients. In his free time he likes to peruse non-fiction books.

He regularly blogs about web development at `www.codediesel.com`.

I would like to thank my wife for her support in all of my different endeavors, even at times when they were impractical. Also thanks to Packt Publishing for providing me with this great learning opportunity. And finally thanks to the Open Source community for making all of this possible.

Table of Contents

Preface

The Selenium 1.0 Testing Tools Beginner's guide shows developers and testers how to create automated tests using a browser. You'll be able to create tests using Selenium IDE, Selenium Remote Control and Selenium 2 as well. A chapter is completely dedicated to Selenium 2. We will then see how our tests use element locators such as CSS, XPath, and DOM to find elements on the page.

Once all the tests have been created we will have a look at how we can speed up the execution of our tests using Selenium Grid.

What this book covers

Chapter 1, Getting started with Selenium IDE: In this chapter we will have a look at installing Selenium IDE and recording our first tests. We will see what is needed to work against AJAX applications.

Chapter 2, Locators: In this chapter we will see how we can find elements on the page to be used in our tests. We will use XPath, CSS, Link Text, and ID to find elements on the page so that we can interact with them.

Chapter 3, Pattern Matching: In this chapter we will have a look at using regular expressions, globbing, and then using the exact text to find elements or test text on the page.

Chapter 4, Using JavaScript: Sometimes it is good to inject JavaScript into the page to improve its testability. There are frameworks that people are using within web applications that don't allow Selenium direct access, so this chapter will explain what we need to do in such cases.

Chapter 5, User-Extensions and Add-ons: This chapter will show us how we can create our own Selenium commands that can be used within Selenium IDE. We will also have a look at creating Add-ons for Selenium IDE to expand the functionality of the Selenium IDE.

Chapter 6, First Steps with Selenium RC: In this chapter we will see how we can set up Selenium Remote Control. We can start running our Selenium IDE tests against browsers that we haven't used yet.

Chapter 7, Creating Selenium Remote Control Tests: In the previous chapter we had a look at getting our tests running against different browsers. This chapter goes one step further so we can convert our IDE tests to use a programming language. We also have a look at some good practices and how to integrate with a CI Server.

Chapter 8, Advanced Selenium Techniques: In this chapter we will have a look at how we can do cookie handling within our tests. We will also have a look at how we can create our own locator strategies for find elements on the page. We then move to capturing network traffic between the browser and the web server. We finish off capturing screenshots and video.

Chapter 9, Getting started with Selenium Grid: This chapter shows us how we can set up our Selenium Grid. Selenium Grid is a very good infrastructural tool for managing Selenium Remote Control instances so we run tests against it.

Chapter 10, Running Selenium Tests in parallel: Selenium tests generally run sequentially. This chapter demonstrates how we can use TestNG to run our tests in parallel to take full advantage of Selenium Grid.

Chapter 11, Getting started with Selenium 2: This chapter will help explain the merger of Selenium and WebDriver to create Selenium 2. It explains how the interaction with the browser has changed and how we can convert our Selenium 1 tests to Selenium 2 in order to take advantage of these changes. Finally, we have a look at how executing JavaScript has changed.

What you need for this book

- Mozilla Firefox
- Google Chrome
- Internet Explorer
- Intellij IDEA
- Firebug
- Firefinder
- Selenium IDE
- Selenium Remote Control
- Selenium Grid
- Ubuntu Linux

Who this book is for

If you are a software quality assurance professional, software project manager, or software developer interested in developing automated testing in web-based applications, then this book is definitely for you.

Conventions

In this book, you will find several headings appearing frequently.

To give clear instructions of how to complete a procedure or task, we use:

Time for action – heading

1. Action 1
2. Action 2
3. Action 3

Instructions often need some extra explanation so that they make sense, so they are followed with:

What just happened?

This heading explains the working of tasks or instructions that you have just completed.

You will also find some other learning aids in the book, including:

Pop quiz – heading

These are short multiple choice questions intended to help you test your own understanding.

Have a go hero – heading

These set practical challenges and give you ideas for experimenting with what you have learned.

You will also find a number of styles of text that distinguish between different kinds of information. Here are some examples of these styles, and an explanation of their meaning.

Code words in text are shown as follows: "We can include other contexts through the use of the `include` directive."

A block of code is set as follows:

```
@Before

public void someMethodName(){

    selenium.doSomething();

    selenium.doSomethingElse();

}
```

When we wish to draw your attention to a particular part of a code block, the relevant lines or items are set in bold:

```
@Before

public void someMethodName(){

    selenium.doSomething();
    selenium.doSomethingElse();

}
```

Any command-line input or output is written as follows:

```
-jar selenium-server-standalone.jar
```

New terms and **important words** are shown in bold. Words that you see on the screen, in menus or dialog boxes for example, appear in the text like this: "clicking the **Next** button moves you to the next screen".

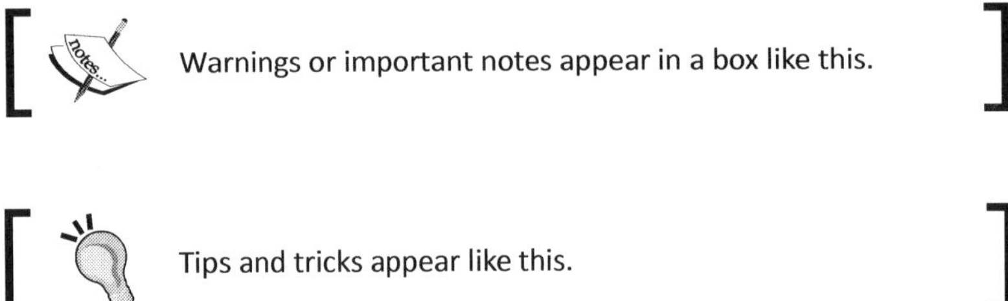

Warnings or important notes appear in a box like this.
Tips and tricks appear like this.

Reader feedback

Feedback from our readers is always welcome. Let us know what you think about this book—what you liked or may have disliked. Reader feedback is important for us to develop titles that you really get the most out of.

To send us general feedback, simply send an e-mail to `feedback@packtpub.com`, and mention the book title via the subject of your message.

If there is a book that you need and would like to see us publish, please send us a note in the **SUGGEST A TITLE** form on `www.packtpub.com` or e-mail `suggest@packtpub.com`.

If there is a topic that you have expertise in and you are interested in either writing or contributing to a book, see our author guide on `www.packtpub.com/authors`.

Errata

Although we have taken every care to ensure the accuracy of our content, mistakes do happen. If you find a mistake in one of our books—maybe a mistake in the text or the code—we would be grateful if you would report this to us. By doing so, you can save other readers from frustration and help us improve subsequent versions of this book. If you find any errata, please report them by visiting `http://www.packtpub.com/support`, selecting your book, clicking on the **errata submission form** link, and entering the details of your errata. Once your errata are verified, your submission will be accepted and the errata will be uploaded on our website, or added to any list of existing errata, under the Errata section of that title. Any existing errata can be viewed by selecting your title from `http://www.packtpub.com/support`.

Piracy

Piracy of copyright material on the Internet is an ongoing problem across all media. At Packt, we take the protection of our copyright and licenses very seriously. If you come across any illegal copies of our works, in any form, on the Internet, please provide us with the location address or website name immediately so that we can pursue a remedy.

Please contact us at `copyright@packtpub.com` with a link to the suspected pirated material.

We appreciate your help in protecting our authors, and our ability to bring you valuable content.

Questions

You can contact us at `questions@packtpub.com` if you are having a problem with any aspect of the book, and we will do our best to address it.

1

Getting Started with Selenium IDE

Test automation has grown in popularity over the years because teams do not have the time or money to invest in large test teams to make sure that applications work as they are expected to. Developers also want to make sure that the code they have created works as they expect it to.

Developers use a multitude of different testing frameworks to test different aspects of the system. Selenium is one of the most well-known testing frameworks in the world that is in use. It is an open source project that allows testers and developers alike to develop functional tests to drive the browser. It can be used to record workflows so that developers can prevent future regressions of code. Selenium can work on any browser that supports JavaScript since Selenium has been built using JavaScript.

In this chapter, we will cover the following topics:

- What is Selenium IDE
- Recording our first test
- Updating tests to work with AJAX sites
- Using variables in our tests
- Debugging tests
- Saving tests to be used later
- Creating and saving test suites

So let's get on with it...

Important preliminary points

Before we start working through this chapter you need to make sure that Mozilla Firefox is installed on your machine. If you do not have Mozilla Firefox installed, you will need to download it from `http://www.getfirefox.com/`.

What is Selenium IDE

Selenium IDE is a Firefox add-on developed originally by *Shinya Kasatani* as a way to use the original Selenium Core without having to copy Selenium Core onto the server. It has been developed using JavaScript so that it can interact with DOM (Document Object Model) using native JavaScript calls.

Selenium IDE was developed to allow testers and developers to record their actions as they follow the workflow that they need to test.

Time for action – installing Selenium IDE

Now that we understand what Selenium IDE is, it is a good time to install the Selenium IDE. By the end of these steps, you will have successfully installed the Selenium IDE on your computer.

1. Go to `http://seleniumhq.org/download/`.
2. Click on the download link for Selenium IDE. You may get a message saying **Firefox prevented this site (seleniumhq.org) from asking you to install software on your computer**. If you do, click on the **Allow** button.
3. A pop up will appear, as seen in the next screenshot:

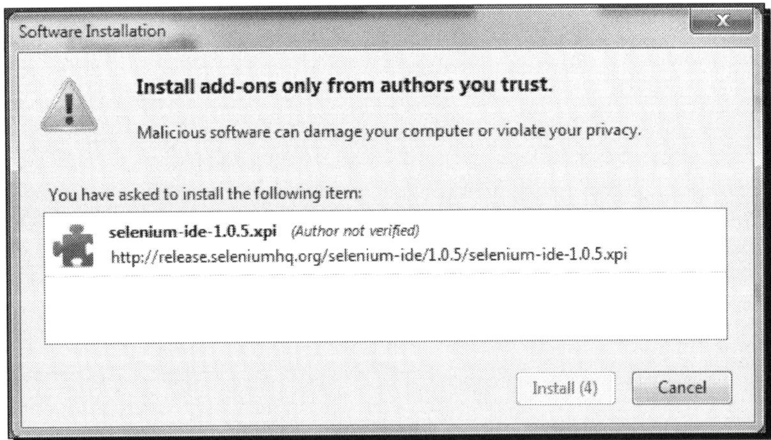

4. Once the countdown has finished, the **Install** button will become active and you can click on it. This will now install the Selenium IDE as a Firefox add-on.

5. Once the installation process is complete, it will ask you to restart Firefox. Click on the **Restart** button. Firefox will close and then reopen. If you have anything open in another browser, it might be worth saving your work as Firefox will try to go back to its original state, but this cannot be guaranteed.

6. Once the installation is complete, the **Add-ons** window will show the Selenium IDE and its current version.

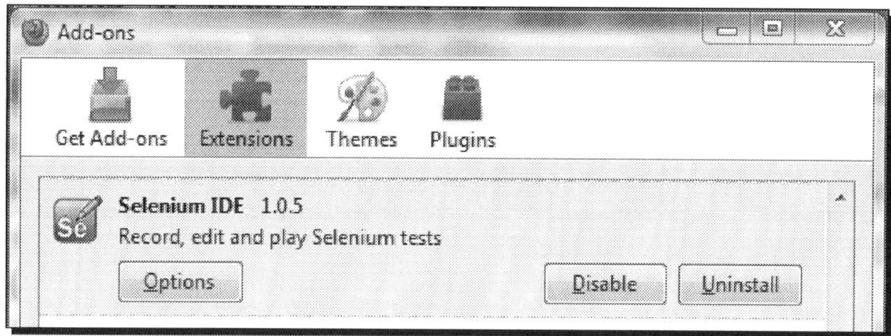

What just happened?

You have successfully installed Selenium IDE, and we can now start thinking about writing our first test.

Selenium IDE

Selenium IDE has been installed, so let's take some time to familiarize ourselves with it. This will give us the foundation that we can use in later chapters.

Open up Selenium IDE by going through the **Tools** menu in Mozilla Firefox. The steps are **Tools | Selenium IDE**. The window that will appear should be similar to the next screenshot.

Selenium IDE icons

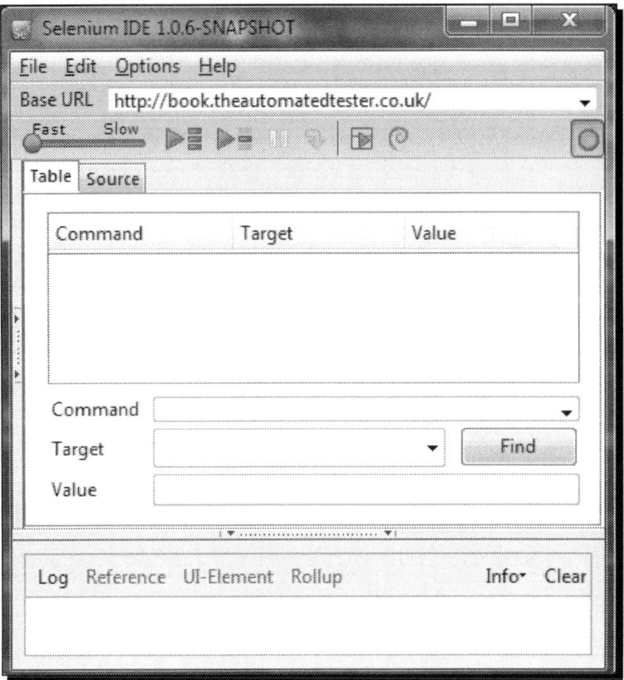

Starting from the top, I will explain what each of the items is:

- **Base URL**—This is the URL that the test will start. All **open** commands will be relative to the Base URL unless a full path is inserted in the **open** command.
- **Speed Slider**—This is the slider under the **Fast Slow** labels on the screen.
- —Run all the tests in the IDE.
- —Run a single test in the IDE.
- —Pause a test that is currently running.
- —Step through the test once it has paused.
- —This is the record button. It will be engaged when the test is recording.

- —This allows you to run your tests using the **Selenium Core TestRunner** and not Selenium IDE. When pressed, it will open up Firefox to the `TestRunner` and it looks similar to the next screenshot:

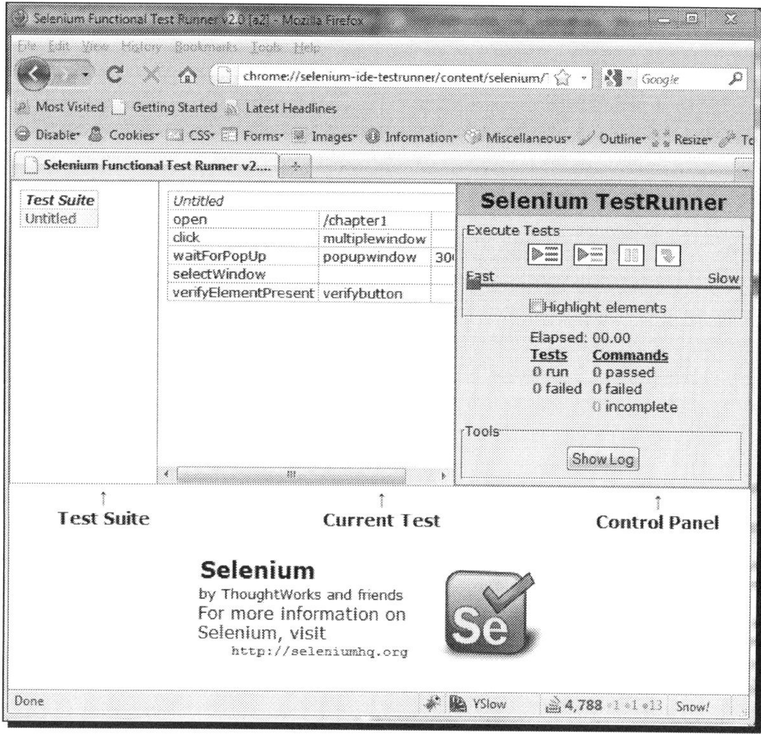

- The Selenese **Command** select box has a list of all the commands that are needed to create a test. You can type into it to use the auto complete functionality or use it as a dropdown.
- **Target** textbox allows you to input the location of the element that you want to work against.
- The **Find** button, once the target box is populated, can be clicked on to highlight the element on the page.
- **Value** textbox is where you place the value that needs to change. For example, if you want your test to type in an input box on the web page, you would put what you want it to type in the value box.

- The **Test** table will keep track of all of your commands, targets, and values. It has been structured this way because the original version of Selenium was styled on FIT tests. The tests were originally designed to be run from HTML files and the IDE keeps this idea for its tests. If you click on the **Source** tab, you will be able to see the HTML that will store the test. Each of the rows will look like:

```
<tr>
  <td>open</td>
  <td>/chapter1</td>
  <td></td>
</tr>
```

- The area below the **Value** textbox will show the Selenium log while the tests are running. If an item fails, then it will have an **[error]** entry. This area will also show help on Selenium commands when you are working in the **Command** select box. This can be extremely useful when typing commands into the Selenium IDE instead of using the record feature.

Important note

Now that we have installed Selenium IDE and understood what it is, we can think about working through our first tests. There are a few things that you need to consider when creating your first test. These rules apply to any form of test automation but need to be adhered to especially when creating tests against a User Interface.

- Tests should always have a known starting point. In the context of Selenium, this could mean opening a certain page to start a workflow.
- Tests should not have to rely on any other tests to run. If a test is going to add something, do not have a separate test to delete it. This is to ensure that if something goes wrong in one test, it will not mean you have a lot of unnecessary failures to check.
- Tests should only test one thing at a time.
- Tests should clean up after themselves.

These rules, like most rules, can be broken. However, breaking them can mean that you may run into issues later on, and when you have hundreds or even thousands of tests, these small issues can mean that large parts of a test suite are red.

With these rules in mind, let us create our first Selenium IDE test.

Time for action – recording your first test with Selenium IDE

We are going to record our first test using Selenium IDE. To start recording the tests, we will need to start Mozilla Firefox. Once it has been loaded, you will need to start the Selenium IDE. You will find it under the **Tools** menu in Mozilla Firefox. Note that the record button is engaged when you first load the IDE.

To start recording your tests:

1. Change the **Base URL** to the Base URL of the application under test. In this exercise, we will do it against `http://book.theautomatedtester.co.uk/`.
2. Click on the radio button.
3. Change the value of the **Select**.
4. Click on the link.

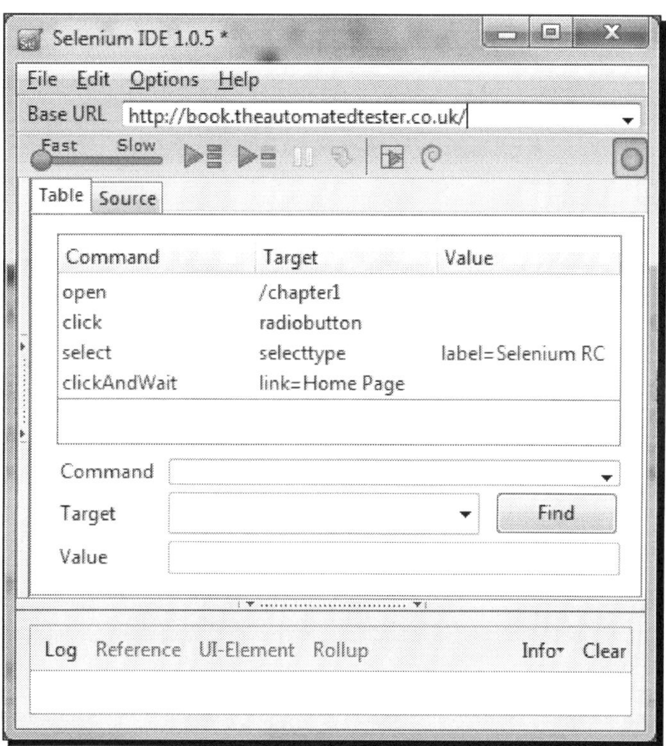

5. Your test has now been recorded and should look the like the previous screenshot. Click on the play button that looks like this: .

6. Once your test has completed, it will look similar to the next screenshot:

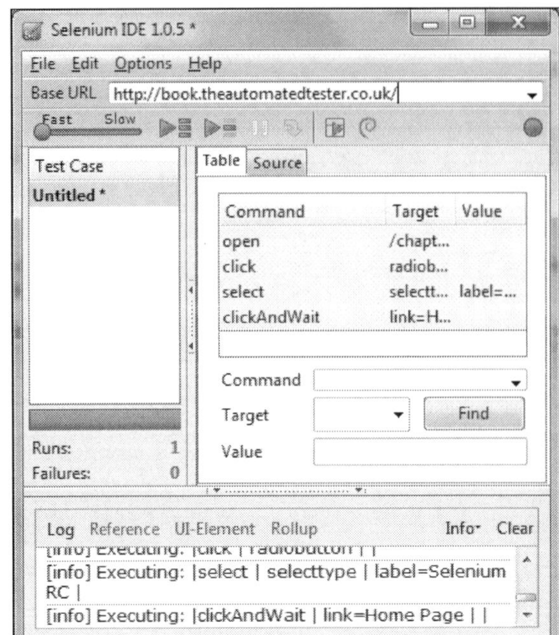

What just happened?

We have successfully been able to record our first test and played it back. As we can see, the Selenium IDE has tried to apply the first rule of test automation by specifying the **open** command. It has set the starting point of the test, in this case `/chapter1`, and then it began stepping through the workflow that we want to record.

Once all the actions have been completed, you will see that all of the actions have a green background. This shows that they have completed successfully. On the left-hand side, you will see that it has completed **1** successful test, or run, that is, in Selenium IDE. If you were to write a test that failed, the **Failures** label would have a **1** next to it.

Pop quiz – Selenium IDE

- What is the main language that drives Selenium IDE?
    - Ruby
    - Python
    - JavaScript

- Selenium IDE works on Internet Explorer.
    - ❑ True
    - ❑ False

Updating a test to assert items are on the page

In the previous steps, we were able to record a workflow that we would expect the user to perform. It will test that the relevant bit of functionality is present, such as buttons and links to work against. Unfortunately, we are not checking that the other items on the page are there or if they are visible when they should be hidden. We are going to work against the same page as before, but we shall make sure that different items are on the page.

There are two mechanisms for validating elements that are available on the application under test. The first is *assert*: this allows the test to check if the element is on the page. If it is not available, then the test will stop on the step that failed. The second is *verify*: this also allows the test to check whether the element is on the page, but if it isn't, then the test will carry on executing.

To add the assert or verify to the tests, we need to use the context menu that Selenium IDE adds to Firefox. All that one needs to do is right-click on the element if on Windows or Linux. If you have a Mac, then you will need to do the two-finger click to display the **Context** menu.

When the **Context** menu appears, it will look like the next screenshot with the normal Firefox functions above it.

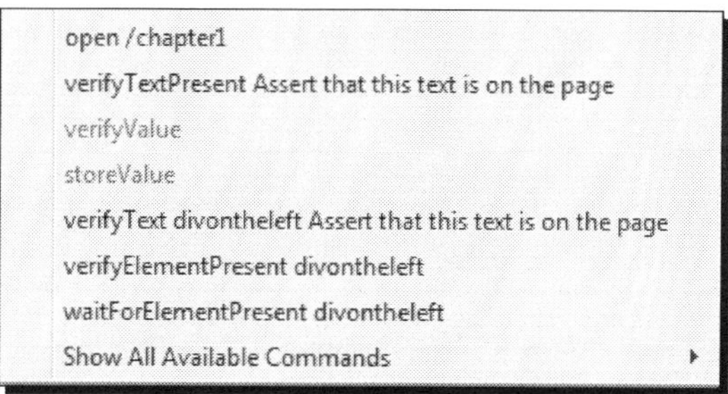

Time for action – updating a test to verify items on the page

1. Open the IDE so that we can start recording.
2. Set the **Base URL** to `http://book.theautomatedtester.co.uk/`.
3. Click on `Chapter1`.
4. Click on the radio button.

5. Change the select to **Selenium Grid**.
6. Verify that the text on the right-hand side of the page has **Assert that this text is on the page**. You can see the command in the previous screenshot.
7. Verify that the button is on the page. You will need to use the context menu for this.
8. Now that you have completed the previous steps, your Selenium IDE should look similar to the next screenshot:

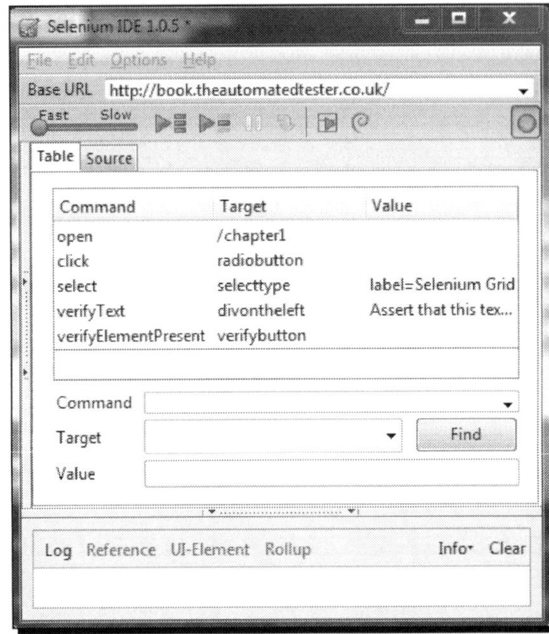

If you now run the test, you will see it has verified that what you are expecting to see on the page has appeared. Notice that the verify commands have a darker green. This is to show that they are more important to the test than moving through the steps. The test has now checked that the text we required is on the page and that the button was there too.

What would happen if the verify command did not find what it was expecting? The IDE would have thrown an error stating what was expected was not there, but it carried on with the rest of the test. We can see an example of this in the next screenshot:

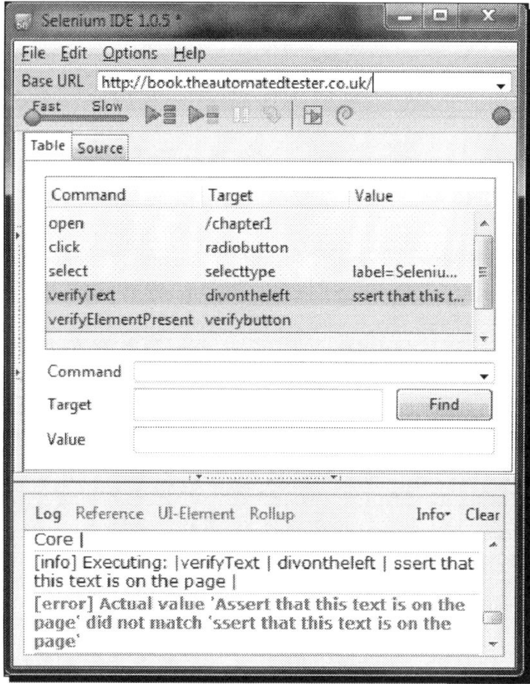

The test would not have carried on if it was using *assert* as the mechanism for validating that the elements and text were loaded with the page.

What just happened?

We have just seen that we can add asserts or verification to the page. Selenium IDE does not do this when recording, so it will always be a manual step. We saw that if we use the assert command and it fails, it will cause the test to stop, whereas the verify command allows the test to carry on after a failure. Each of these has their merits.

Have a go hero – using the IDE

Recreate the test that you have just done but using the assert methods available from the context menu in Firefox.

Some of the verify and assert methods are:

- `verifyElementPresent`
- `verifyElementNotPresent`
- `verifyText`
- `verifyAttribute`

- `verifyChecked`
- `verifyAlert`
- `verifyTitle`

Pop quiz

- Selenium verifies items on the page when it is recording steps.
  - True
  - False
- What is the difference between verify and assert?
- If you wanted to validate that a button, which has appeared, is on a page, what two commands would be the best to use?
  - `verifyTextPresent/assertTextPresent`
  - `verifyElementPresent/assertElementPresent`
  - `verifyAlertPresent/assertAlertPresent`
  - `verifyAlert/assertAlert`

Comments

Before we carry on further with Selenium, it would be a good time to mention how to create comments in your tests. As all good software developers know, having readable code with descriptive comments can make maintenance in the future much easier. Unlike in software development, it is extremely hard, almost impossible, to write self-documenting code. To combat this, it is good practice to make sure that your tests have comments that future software testers can use.

Time for action – adding Selenium IDE comments

To add comments to your tests, use the following steps:

1. In a test that was created earlier, right-click on a step, for example, the verify step.
2. The Selenium IDE context menu will be visible, as seen in the next screenshot:

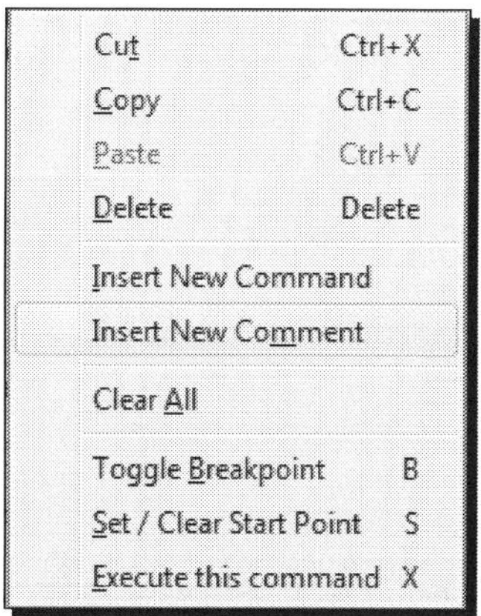

3. Click on the **Insert New Comment.** A space will appear between the Selenium commands.

4. Click on the **Command** textbox and enter in a comment so that you can use it for future maintenance. It will look similar to the next screenshot:

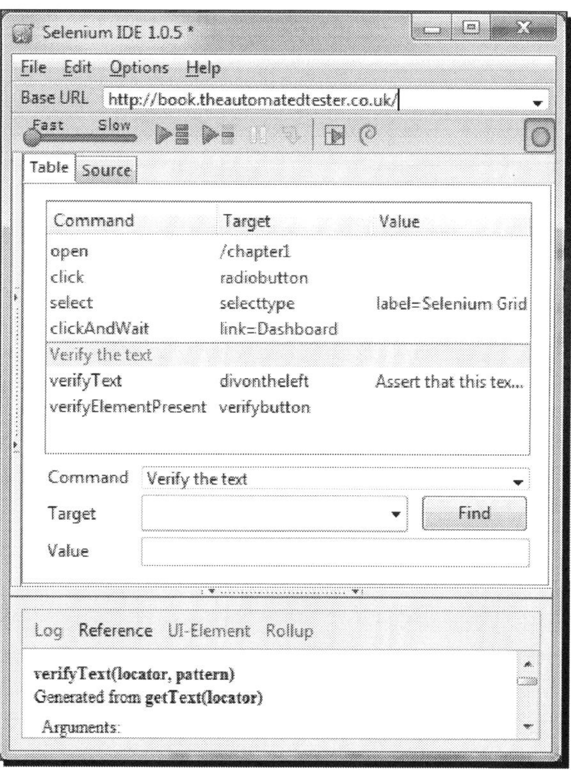

What just happened?

We have just had a look at how to create comments. Comments will always appear as purple text in the IDE. This, like in most IDEs, is to help you spot comments quicker when looking through your test cases. Now that we know how to keep our tests maintainable with comments, let's carry on working with Selenium IDE to record, tweak, or replay our scripts.

Multiple windows

Web applications unfortunately do not live in a single window of your browser. An example of this could be a site that shows reports. Most reports would have their own window so that people can easily move between them.

Unfortunately, in testing terms, this can be quite difficult to do, but in this section we will have a look at creating a test that can move between windows.

Time for action – working with multiple windows

Working with multiple browser windows can be one of the most difficult things to do within a Selenium test. This is down to the fact that the browser needs to allow Selenium to programmatically know how many child browser processes have been spawned.

In the examples given next, we will click on an element on the page, which will cause a new window to appear. If you have a pop-up blocker running, it may be a good idea to disable it for this site while you work through these examples.

1. Open up the Selenium IDE and go to the `Chapter1` page on the site.
2. Click on one of the elements on the page that has the text **Click this link to launch another window**. This will cause a small window to appear.
3. Once the window has loaded, click on the **Close the window** text inside it.
4. Add a *verify* command for an element on the page. Your test should now look similar to the next screenshot.
5. Click on the **Close the window** link.
6. Verify the element on the original window.

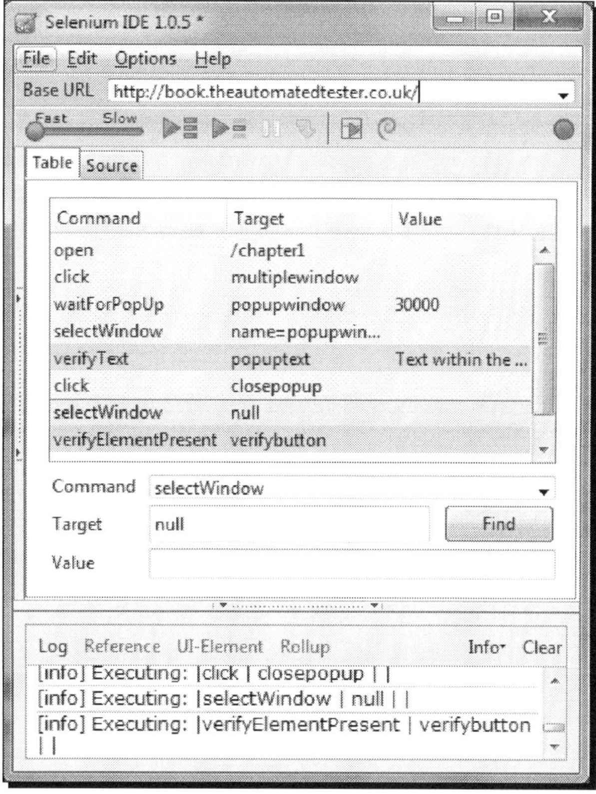

What just happened?

In the test script, we can see that it has clicked on the item to load the new window and then has inserted a **waitForPopUp**. This is so that your test knows that it has to wait for a web server to handle the request and the browser to render the page. Any commands that require a page to load from a web server will have a `waitFor` command.

The next command is the **selectWindow** command. This command tells Selenium IDE that it will need to switch context to the window called **popupwindow** and will execute all the commands that follow in that window unless told otherwise by a later command.

Once the test has finished with the pop-up window, it will need to return to the parent window from where it started. To do this we need to specify **null** as the window. This will force the `selectWindow` to move the context of the test back to its parent window.

Time for action – switching between multiple windows

In the next example, we are going to open up two pop-up windows and move between them and the parent window as it completes its steps.

1. Start the Selenium IDE and go to `Chapter1` on the website.
2. Click on the first link that will launch a pop-up window.
3. Assert the text on the page.
4. Go back to the parent window and click on the link to launch the second pop-up window.
5. Verify the text on the page.
6. Move to the first pop-up window and close it using the close link.
7. Move to the second pop-up window and close it using the close link.
8. Move back to the parent window and verify an element on that page.
9. Run your test and watch how it moves between the windows. When complete, it should look similar to the next screenshot:

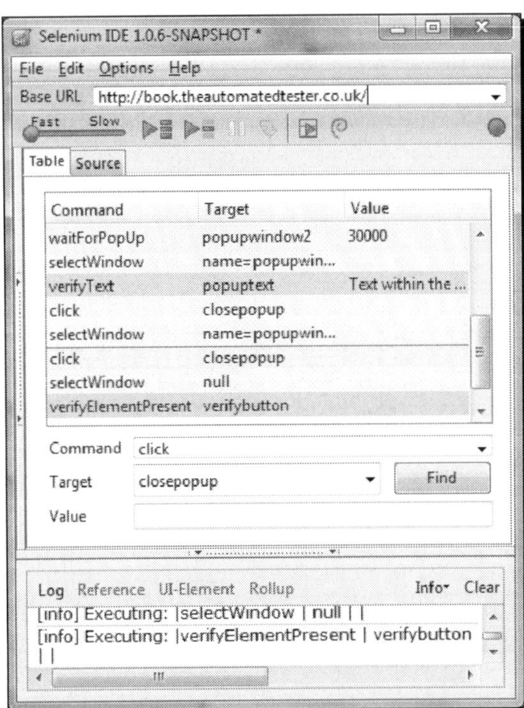

What just happened?

We just had a look at creating a test that can move between multiple windows. We saw how we can move between the child windows and its parent window as though we were a user.

Selenium tests against AJAX applications

Web applications today are being designed in such a way that they appear the same as desktop applications. Web developers are accomplishing this by using AJAX within their web applications. **AJAX** stands for **Asynchronous JavaScript and XML** due to the fact that it relies on JavaScript for creating asynchronous calls and then returning XML with the data that the user or application requires in order to carry on. AJAX does not rely on XML anymore, as more and more people move over to **JavaScript Object Notation** (**JSON**), which is more lightweight in the way that it transfers the data. It does not rely on the extra overhead of opening and closing tags that is needed to create valid XML.

Time for action – working on pages with AJAX

In our first example given next, we are going to click on a link and then assert that some text is visible on the screen:

1. Start up the Selenium IDE and make sure that the **Record** button is pressed.
2. Click on the text that says **Click this link to load a page with AJAX**.
3. Assert the text that appears on your screen. Your test should appear similar to the next screenshot. Selenium IDE will generate all the locators that are needed in this test:

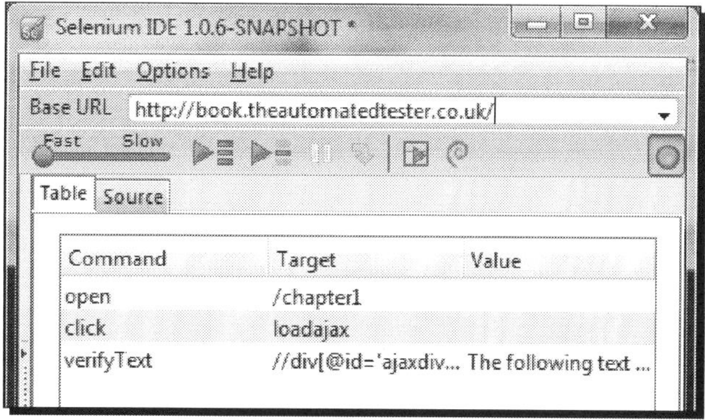

4. Run the test that you have created. When it has finished running, it should look similar to the next screenshot:

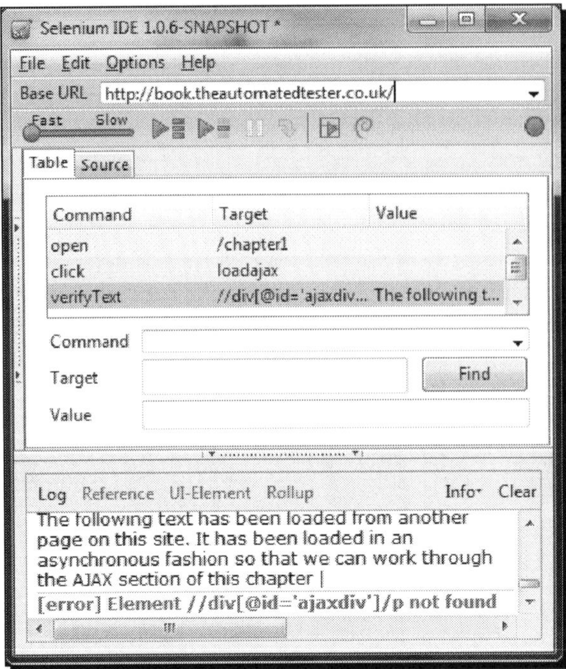

Have a look at the page that you are working against. Can you see the text that the test is expecting? You should see it, then why has this test failed? The test has failed because when the test reached that point, the element containing the text was not loaded into the DOM. This is because it was being requested and rendered from the web server into the browser.

To remedy this issue, we will need to add a new command to our test so that our tests pass in the future.

1. Right-click on the step that failed so that the Selenium IDE context menu appears.
2. Click on **Insert New Command**.
3. In the **Command** select box, type `waitForElementPresent` or select it from the drop-down list.
4. In the **Target** box, add the target that is used in the **verifyText** command.
5. Run the test again, and it should pass this time.

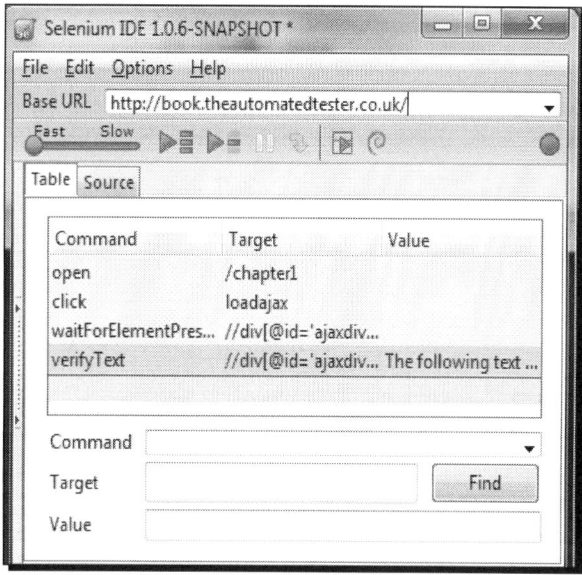

What just happened?

Selenium does not implicitly wait for the item that it needs to interact with, so it is seen as good practice to wait for the item that you need to work with and then interact with it. The `waitFor` commands will timeout after 30 seconds by default, but if you need them to wait longer, you can specify the tests by using the **setTimeout** command. This will set the timeout value that the tests will use in future commands.

Time for action – working with AJAX applications

1. Click on the button that has **load text to the page**.
2. Wait for the text **I have been added with a timeout**. Your test will look similar to the next screenshot:

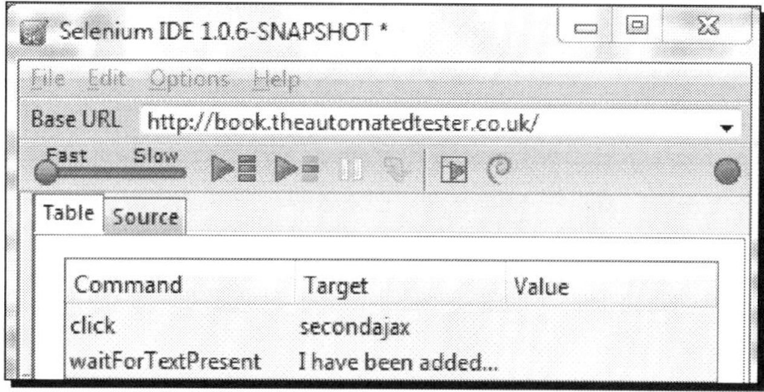

What just happened?

In the previous examples, we waited for an element to appear on the page. There are a number of different commands that we can use to wait. The following commands make up the `waitFor` set of commands, but this is not an exhaustive list:

- `waitForAlertNotPresent`
- `waitForAlertPresent`
- `waitForElementPresent`
- `waitForElementNotPresent`
- `waitForTextPresent`
- `waitForTextNotPresent`
- `waitForPageToLoad`
- `waitForFrameToLoad`

A number of these commands are run implicitly when other commands are being run. An example of this is the `clickAndWait` command. This will fire off a `click` command and then fire off a `waitForPageToLoad`. Another example is the `open` command, which only completes when the page has fully loaded.

If you are feeling confident, then it would be a good time to try different `waitFor` techniques.

Pop quiz – Selenium IDE

- If an element got added after the page has loaded, what command would you use to make sure the test passed in the future?
  - `waitForElementPresent`
  - `pause`
  - `assertElementPresent`

Storing information from the page in the test

Sometimes there is a need to store elements that are on the page to be used later in a test. This could be that your test needs to pick a date that is on the page and use it later so that you do not need to hardcode values into your test.

Once the element has been stored, you will be able to use it again by requesting it from a JavaScript dictionary that Selenium keeps track of. To use the variable, it will take one of the following two formats: it can look like `${variableName}` or `storedVars['variableName']`. I prefer the `storedVars` format, as it follows the same format because it is within Selenium internals.

Time for action – storing elements from the page

To see how this works, let's work through the following example:

1. Open the Selenium IDE and switch off the **Record** button.
2. Right-click on the text **Assert that this text is on the page**, go to the **storeText** command in the context menu, and click on it. If it does not display there, go to **Show all Available Commands** and click on it there.
3. A dialog will appear similar to the next screenshot. Enter the name of a variable that you want to use. I have used `textOnThePage` as the name of my variable.

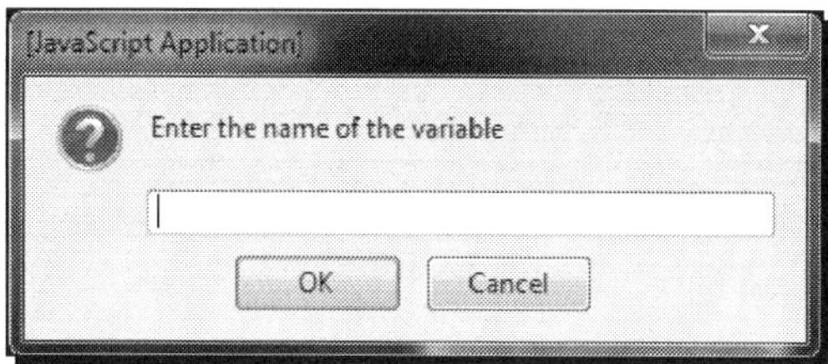

4. Click on the row below the **storeText** command in Selenium IDE.
5. Type the command `type` into the **Command** textbox.
6. Type `storeinput` into the target box.
7. Type `javascript{storedVars['textOnThePage'];}` into the value box.
8. Run the test. It should look similar to the next screenshot:

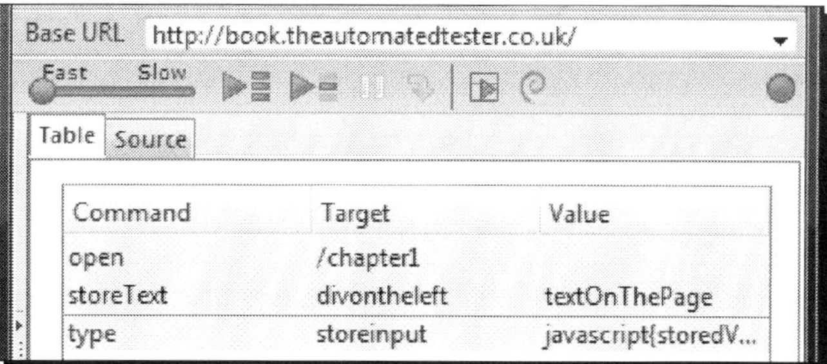

What just happened?

Once your test has completed running, you will see that it has placed **Assert that this text is on the page** into the textbox.

Debugging tests

We have successfully created a number of tests and have seen how we can work against AJAX applications, but unfortunately creating tests that run perfectly first time can be difficult. Sometimes, as a test automater, you will need to debug your tests to see what is wrong.

To work through this part of the chapter, you will need to have a test open in the Selenium IDE.

Time for action – debugging tests

These two steps are quite useful when your tests are not running and you want to execute a specific command.

1. Highlight a command.
2. Press the *X* key: This will make the command execute in the Selenium IDE.

What just happened?

When a test is running, you can click on the **Pause** button to pause the test after the step that is currently being run. Once the test has been paused, the **Step** button is no longer disabled and you can click on it to step through the test as if you were stepping through an application.

If you are having issues with elements on the page, you can type in their location and then click on the **Find** button. This will surround the element that you are looking for with a green border that flashes for a few seconds.

The `echo` command is also a good way to write something from your test to the log. This is equivalent to `Console.log` in JavaScript.

Test suites

We have managed to create a number of tests using Selenium IDE and have managed to run them successfully. The next thing to have a look at is how to create a test suite. We can open the test suite and then have it run a number of tests that we have created.

Time for action – creating test suites

If you have the Selenium IDE open from the previous steps, click on the **File** menu.

1. Click on **New Test Case**.
2. You will see that Selenium IDE has opened a new area on the left-hand side of the IDE, as seen in the next screenshot:

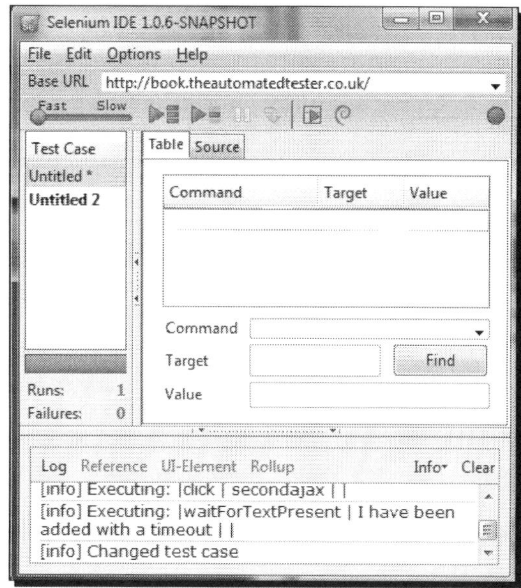

You can do this as many times as you want, and when the **Run Entire Test Suite** button is clicked, it will run all the tests in the test suite. It will log all the passes and failures at the bottom of the **Test Case** box.

To save this, click on the **File** menu and then click on **Save Test Suite** and save the Test Suite file to somewhere convenient.

Changing the name of the test case to something a lot more meaningful, this can be done by right-clicking on the test and clicking on the **Properties** item in the context menu.

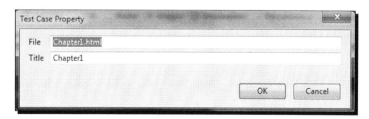

You can now add meaningful names to your tests and they will appear in the Selenium IDE instead of falling back to their filenames.

What just happened?

We have managed to create our first test suite. This can be used to group tests together to be used later. If your tests have been saved, you can update the test suite properties to give the tests a name that is easier to read.

Pop quiz

- How do we run all the tests in a Test Suite?

Saving tests

Saving tests is done in the same manner as saving a test suite. Click on the **File** menu and then click on **Save Test Case**. This will give you a save dialog, save this somewhere that you can access later. When you save your tests and your test suite, Selenium IDE will try to keep the relationships between the folders in step when saving the tests and the test suites.

What you cannot record

We have seen our tests work really well by recording them and then playing them back. Unfortunately, there are a number of things that Selenium cannot do. Since Selenium was developed in JavaScript, it tries to synthesize what the user does with JavaScript events. However, this does mean that it is bound by the same rules that JavaScript has in any browsers by operating within the sandbox.

- Silverlight and Flex/Flash applications, at the time of writing this, cannot be recorded with Selenium IDE. Both these technologies operate in their own sandbox and do not operate with the DOM to do their work.
- HTML5, at the time of writing this, is not fully supported with Selenium IDE. A good example of this is elements that have the `contentEditable=true` attribute. If you want to see this, you can use the type command to type something into the `html5div` element. The test will tell you that it has completed the command but the UI will not have changed, as shown in the next screenshot:

- Selenium IDE does not work with Canvas elements on the page either, so you will not be able to make your tests move items around on a page.
- Selenium cannot do file uploads. This is due to the JavaScript sandbox not allowing JavaScript to interact with `<input type=file>` elements on a page. The tests will be able to insert text, but will not be able to click on the buttons.

Have a go hero – doing more with Selenium IDE

By now you should be feeling rather confident about using Selenium IDE. Try creating a test against your favorite web application. Try to record a test again making sure to add verifications along the way so that your test does what you expect. Run the test and have it pass.

Now try creating the same test by typing in the commands needed to create the test. Have you created a better test by hand or by using the record/tweak and playback?

Summary

We learned a lot in this chapter about Selenium IDE, learning how to create your first test using the record and replay button, and understanding some of the basic concepts such as moving between multiple windows that can appear in a test, and to save our tests for future use.

Specifically, we covered the following topics:

- **How to install Selenium IDE**: We started by downloading Selenium IDE from `http://seleniumhq.org`.
- **What the Selenium IDE is made up of**: The breakup of Selenium IDE allowed us to see what makes up the Selenium IDE. It allowed us to understand the different parts that make up a command that will be executed in a test as well as its basic format.
- **Recording and replaying tests**: Using the Selenium IDE to record a workflow that a user will do through their tests. We also had a look at verifying and asserting that elements are on the page and that the text we are expecting is also on the page.

- **How to add comments to tests**: In this section of the chapter, we saw how to add comments to the tests so that they are more maintainable.
- **Working with multiple windows**: Applications today can have pop-up windows that tests need to be able to move between.
- **Working with AJAX applications**: AJAX applications do not have the items needed for the tests when the tests get to commands. To get around this, we had a look at adding `waitFor` commands to the tests. This is due to the fact that Selenium does not implicitly wait for elements to appear in the page.
- **Storing information in variables**: There is always something that is on the page that needs to be used later, but unfortunately you will not know what the value is before the test runs. This section showed us how we can record items into a variable and use it later in a test.
- **Debugging tests**: Creating tests does not always go according to plan, so in this section we saw some of the different ways to debug your tests.
- **Saving test suites**: Finally we saw how we can save tests for future use, and how we can save them into different groups by saving them into test suites.

We also discussed what cannot be tested using Selenium IDE. We saw that Silverlight and Flex/Flash applications could not be tested and that when working with a number of HTML5 elements, the tests say that they have completed the tasks even though the UI has not changed. In later chapters, we will discuss different mechanisms that we can use within our tests that might be useful against HTML5 elements on the page. Remember that if you do get stuck, you can always have a look at `http://seleniumhq.org/docs/`, which holds the official documentation.

Now that we've learned about Selenium IDE, we're ready to look at all the different techniques to find elements on the page—which is the topic of the next chapter.

2
Locators

Locators allow us to find elements on a page that can be used in our tests. In the previous chapter, we managed to work against a page that had decent locators. In HTML, it is seen as good practice to make sure that every element you need to interact with has an `id` *and a* `name` *attribute. Unfortunately, following best practices can be extremely difficult, especially when building the HTML dynamically on the server before sending it back to the browser.*

In this chapter, we shall:

- Locate elements by ID
- Locate elements by name
- Locate elements by link
- Locate elements by XPath
- Locate elements by CSS

So let's get on with it...

Important preliminary points

Before starting this chapter we should begin by making sure that we have all the relevant applications installed. While these are not foolproof, they will give us some clue of how to construct the locator for our tests to use.

- **Firebug:** `https://addons.mozilla.org/en-US/firefox/addon/1843`
  - Firebug has become the de facto tool for web developers, as it allows developers to find elements on the page by using the find functionality.
  - It has a JavaScript REPL. **REPL** stands for **Read-Eval-Print-Loop**, which is an interactive shell that allows you to run JavaScript without having to create an entire page.
- **Firefinder:** `https://addons.mozilla.org/en-US/firefox/addon/11905`
  - A very good tool for testing out XPath and CSS on the page. It will highlight all the elements on the page that match the selector to your element location.
- **IE Developer Tools**
  - This is built into IE7 and IE8, which we can launch by pressing *F12*. It also has a number of features that Firebug has.
- **Google Chrome Developer Tools**
  - This, like IE, is built into the browser and will also allow you to find the elements on the page and be able to work out its XPath.

Once you have worked out your locator, you will need to put it into the Selenium IDE to test it. At the beginning of Chapter 1, *Getting Started with Selenium IDE*, there was a section that explained the layout of Selenium IDE. One of the buttons on the page is named **Find**. Click on this button when you have something in the **Value** textbox; it will highlight the item in green as seen in the next screenshot:

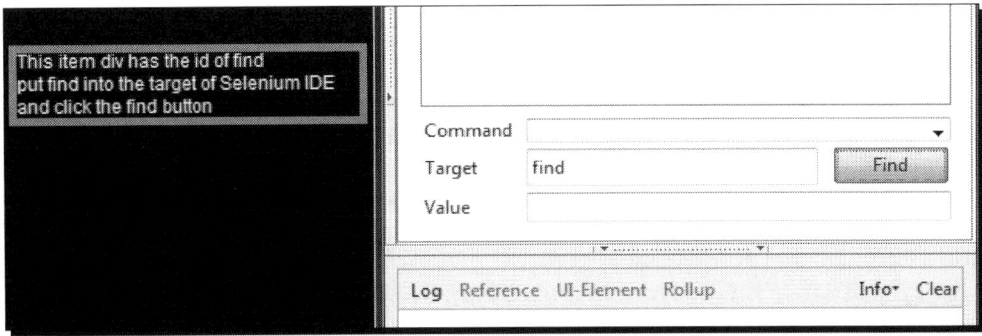

Now that we have these tools and understand how to use them, we can start adding decent locators to our test scripts.

Locating elements by ID

On web applications today, elements will have an ID attribute for all their buttons. This allows Selenium to find the unique item, as IDs should be unique, and then complete the action that it needs to do against that element.

Time for action – finding IDs of elements on the page with Firebug

In this section, we are going to find a number of elements that are on the page. You will need to have Firebug installed for this. We are going to look at how to find the ID of an element using Firefox.

1. Click on the Firebug icon. This is the bug icon on the bottom of Firefox.
2. Click on the icon to the left-hand side of **Console** .
3. Move your mouse over the element that you wish to have a look at.
4. Move your mouse over different elements. As you see in the next screenshot, Firebug will highlight each of the items that you want to see.

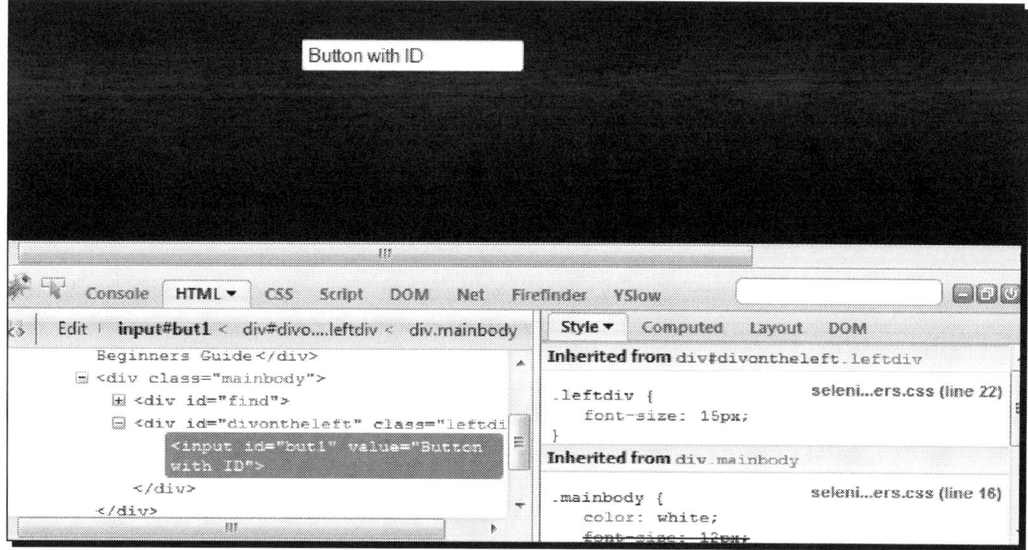

What just happened?

Once the element has been selected, you can see that its different attributes are now visible.

Now that we are confident of how to find elements and their attributes, let's start using them in Selenium.

Pop quiz – using the Find button

- What color is an element bordered with when the **Find** button is clicked in the Selenium IDE?
  - Red
  - Green
  - Amber

Time for action – finding elements by ID

Elements often have IDs that are used to locate them. In the **Target** text box, this would look like `id=element`. Follow the next example to see how it would work:

1. Open Selenium.
2. Open Firebug.
3. Find an element that you want to interact with and in the **Target** box place its ID attribute value. For example, use `but1` as seen in the previous screenshot against `http://book.theautomatedtester.co.uk/chapter2`.
4. Type the command `click` into the **Command** selectbox.
5. Run your script.

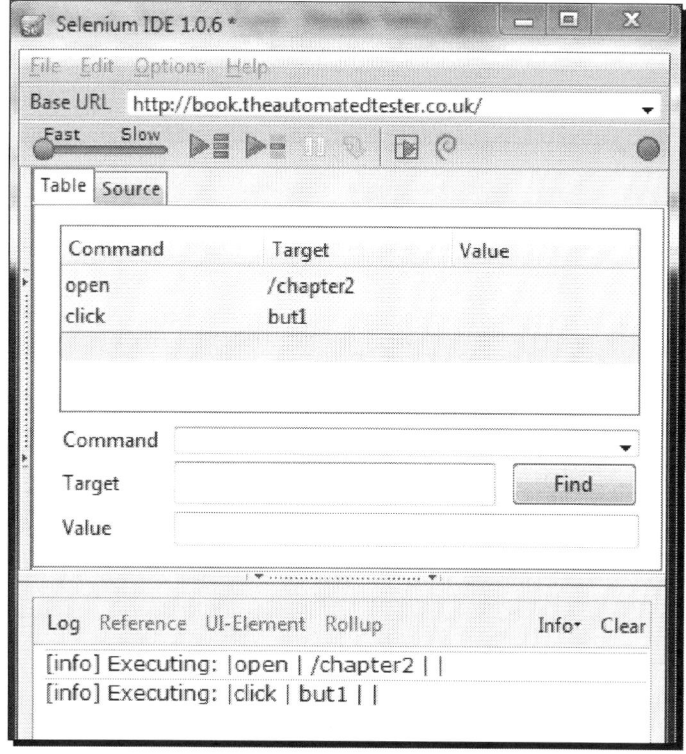

What just happened?

Your test will have executed the step successfully. Because the test is using the ID of the element, if that element were to be moved around, your script would find the item without any issue. This is one of the main plus points of Selenium over a lot of the competing test frameworks out there.

Moving elements on the page

As I just mentioned, when using the value of the ID attribute, Selenium can find the elements on the page even if they were to be moved. Click on the **Random** button in the `chapter2` page of the site (you can do this manually) and then run the script that we created earlier. You will see that your test executes successfully.

Time for action – finding elements by name

Elements do not necessarily have name attributes on all of them. Elements can have names that we can use to locate them. In the **Target** textbox this would look like `name=Element`. Follow the next example to see how it would work:

1. Open Selenium.
2. Open Firebug.
3. Find an element that you want to interact with and in the **Target** textbox place the value of its name attribute. For example, use `verifybutton` as in the next screenshot, against `http://book.theautomatedtester.co.uk/chapter2`.

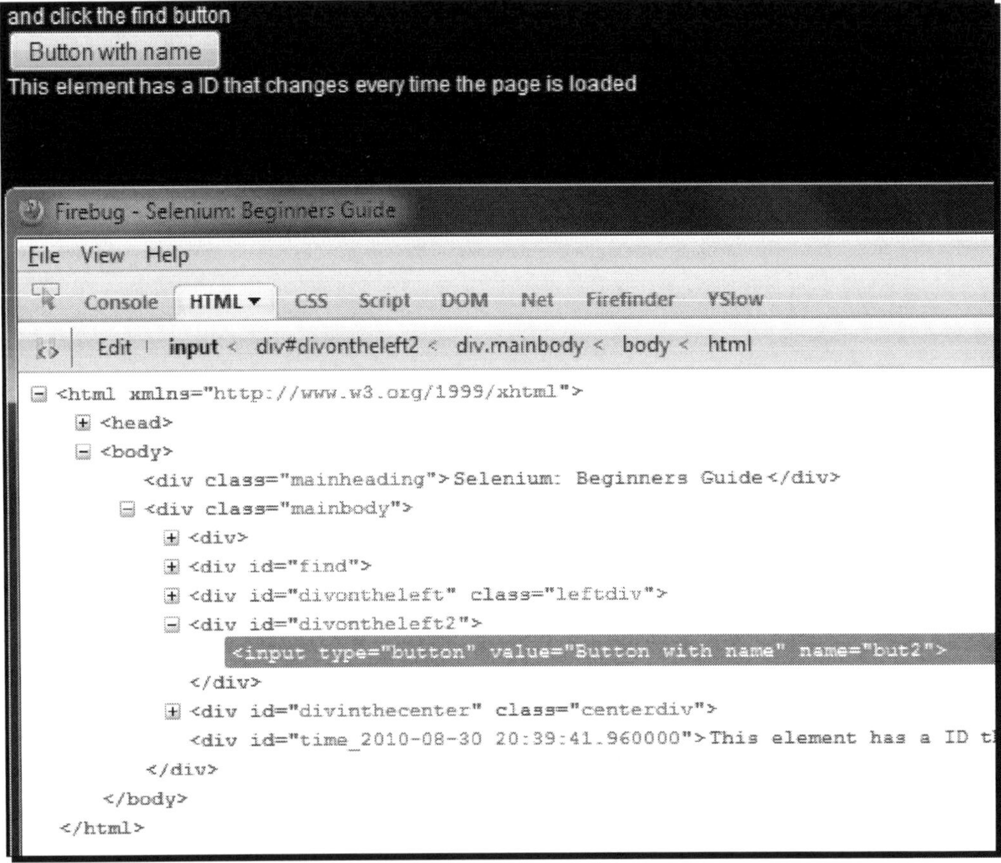

4. Type the command `click` into the **Command** selectbox.
5. Run your script.

What just happened?

Your test will have executed the step successfully. As the test is using the name of the element, if that element were to be moved around, it would find the item without any issue.

Adding filters to the name

There are times that there may be elements on the page that have the same name but a different attribute. When this happens, we can apply filters to the locator so that it can find the element that we are looking for.

An example of this on the page would be `name=verifybutton value=chocolate;`. This will find the second button with the name `verifybutton`. See an example of this in the next screenshot:

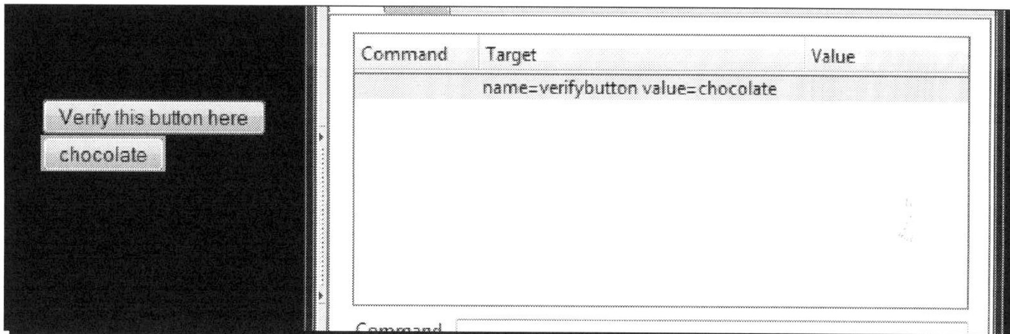

Time for action – finding elements by link text

Probably the most common element on a page is a link. Links allow pages to be joined together so that end users can navigate your site with ease. You can see a screenshot of the element being found in Selenium IDE next.

1. To specify that you want to follow a link, you would use the `target link=link`.
2. Verify a link by using `verifyElementPresent`.

3. On the `chapter2` page, there is a link to the `index` page of the site.

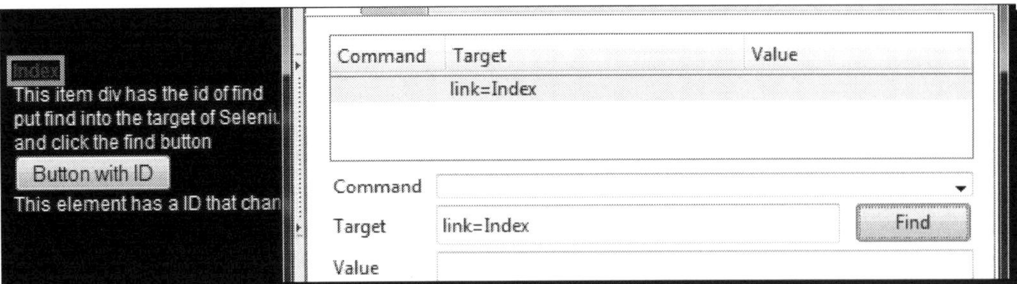

What just happened?

We have seen how we can find links that are on that page so that they can be used in your test. All that is needed is the inner text of the nodes in the DOM.

Time for action – finding elements by accessing the DOM through JavaScript

There are times where the DOM will be updated through AJAX and this means that our locator needed for the test will need some form of JavaScript to see if it is there. In JavaScript, calling the DOM to find the first link on the page would look like `document.links[0];`. On the `chapter2` page of the website, it will show the link that we used in the previous section of this chapter.

This technique is commonly used with the **waitForCondition** command, so it may use fairly simple JavaScript or fairly tricky JavaScript to find the element. So if you needed an ID to be made up of a number of different things, create a function to create that data and then return it.

For example, if you find an element by a regular expression, it would look something like the code given next:

```
function searchLinks (){
  var links = document.links,
  h = new RegExp(/http:\/\//);
  for (link in links){
    if (link.toString().match(h)) { return link; }
  }
}
searchLinks();
```

But normally it will just be calls to the DOM to see if an element has been added such as in the next screenshot.

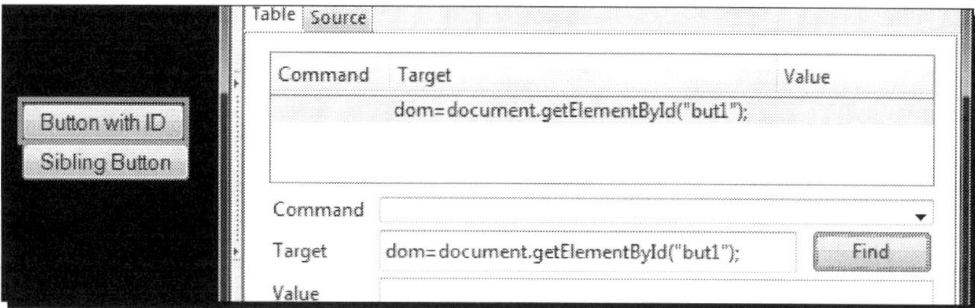

What just happened?

We have just seen that we can use JavaScript to find elements on the page. This can be extremely useful if you have a web application that does a lot of interaction with the DOM.

Pop quiz

- If you wanted to use JavaScript to find the element on the page, which strategy would you use to find it?
    - ID
    - Name
    - DOM
    - CSS selector
    - XPath

Time for action – finding elements by XPath

Unfortunately, best practices cannot always be followed when building the markup, or if they are, they may have a dynamic edge to them. An example of this would be working against a page that uses a key from the database as the element ID. So when something is edited and stored back in the database, it can be found a lot quicker and updated. In this section of the chapter, we are going to work with XPath. XPath allows us to query the DOM as though it were an XML document. With XPath we can do some rather complex queries to find elements on the page that may not have been accessible otherwise.

Let's start by creating a basic XPath. We are going to look for an input button.

1. Open the Selenium IDE.
2. Enter `click` into the **Command** selectbox.

3. Enter `xpath=//input` into the **Target** box.
4. Run your test. It will find a button on the page, as seen in the next screenshot:

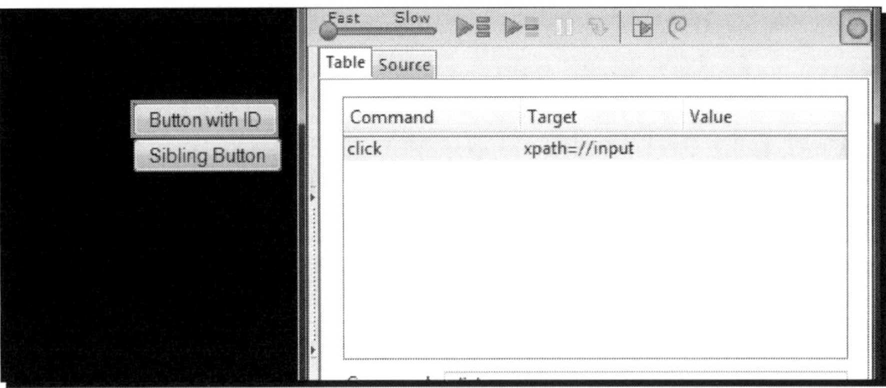

What just happened?

Your test will have looked against the DOM to find an element that was of the type `input`. The `xpath=` at the beginning tells Selenium that the element needed will be located by XPath. It removes the guess work that Selenium would have to do and is seen as good practice. The `//` tells the query that it needs to stop at the first element that it finds. It is a greedy query, so if you have a rather large web page, it can take some time to return since it will try to parse the page. Writing the XPath like this allows us to make changes to the UI, within reason, and not have it impact the test.

Using direct XPath in your test

As I mentioned in the first part of this section, having `//` as the start of your XPath is seen as a greedy query because it will parse the entire DOM until it finds the element that you want to find. If you want to work against an element that will always be in a certain place, you can use a more direct XPath. Instead of using the `//`, you can use a single `/`, but you will need to make sure that the first node in your query is HTML. Let's see an example of this.

1. Open the Selenium IDE.
2. Enter `xpath=/html/body/div[2]/div[3]/input`.
3. Click on the **Find** button.

The given locator will have found the same element as before. This type of XPath query will find the element fractionally quicker, but if your UI is going to change, it may fail if the element is moved into a different area of the page.

You will have noticed that parent and child nodes are in the same query. Because HTML has a tree structure, it just notifies the query that it needs to start at the `html` node and then move to its child node, `body`, and then to the body's child and so on until it reaches the end of the query. Once it has done that, it will stop executing the query.

Using XPath to find the nth element of a type

There are a lot of occasions where, as a Selenium user, you will have to click on an edit button in a table so that you can update something specific. Have a look at the button that you wish to click—it does not have a unique name or ID.

When running a query against the DOM, an array of elements is returned to Selenium that matches the query. For example, if you were to run `//div` on the `chapter2` page of the website, there are three elements returned to Selenium. If your test is only relying on the first item in your test, then it will try to access only the first item. If you wanted to interact with the second element, then your query would look like `//div[2]`. Note that the second to nth element needs to be sibling nodes of the first element that is returned. If they are not and you were to access the element, it would fail saying that it could not find them.

We can see this with the input buttons that are present on the page. They all reside in their own containing `div` element, so do not have any sibling elements that are also input elements. If you were to enter `//input[2]` into the Selenium IDE, it would not be able to find the element and fail. You can see an example of this in the next screenshot:

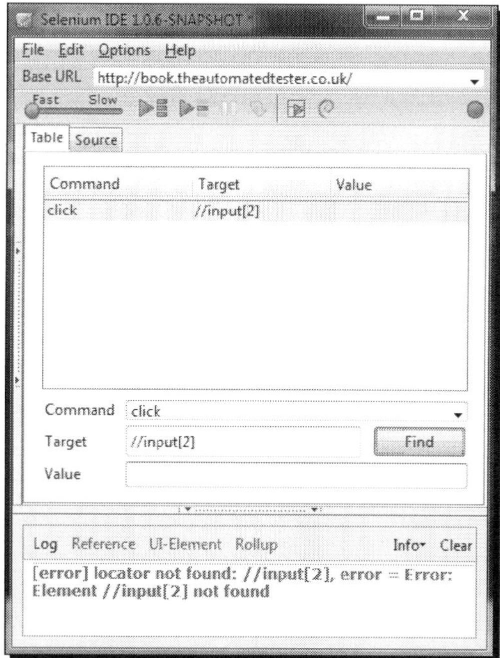

Using element attributes in XPath queries

There are times that you will need to find elements that are the same except for the difference in one or two attributes. To handle this, we can add the attributes to the query so that we can try to make the element more unique for use in the test. The format can be used for any attribute on any element. It will always follow the `xpath=//element[@attribute='attribute value']`. For example, if you have two div elements on the page but they only differ by the `class` attribute, your XPath query would look like `xpath=//div[@class='classname']`.

Try doing this with Selenium yourself by trying to identify something unique about the div elements on the page. When you have completed the task, your query should look like one in the next screenshot:

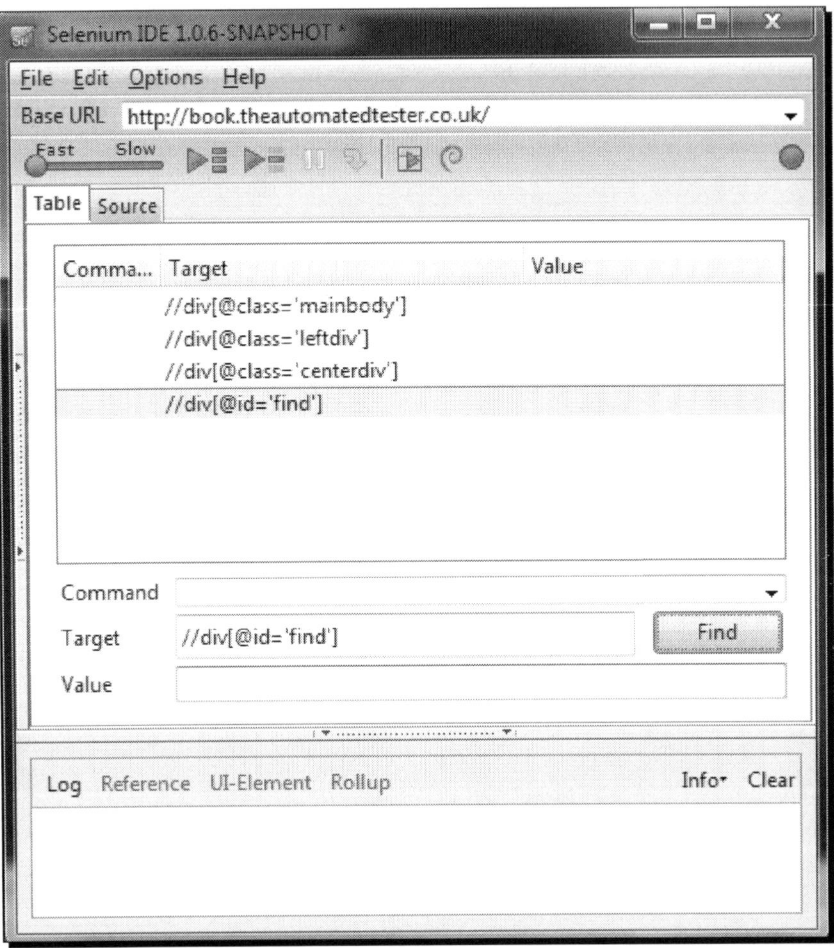

Doing a partial match on attribute content

As mentioned earlier, there are times where there is no way for a developer to create a static ID for elements on the page. This could be down to the fact that the element is being loaded asynchronously through AJAX or because it is using the key of the data as it is stored in the database.

There are times where only part of the ID is dynamic. This is to allow the developer to cram more information onto the page so that the user has everything they need. We will need to have a mechanism to work with these elements.

To do the partial match, your query will need to have the word `contains` with the attribute and the partial match that it needs. For example, if you wanted to access the element that has the text "**This element has an ID that changes every time the page is loaded**" in it, you will use `//div[contains(@id,'time_')]`. This is due to the first part of the ID always being static. The locator could also use `starts-with` instead of `contains` to make the XPath query stricter in what is returned. The queries in the next screenshot will find the same element on the page:

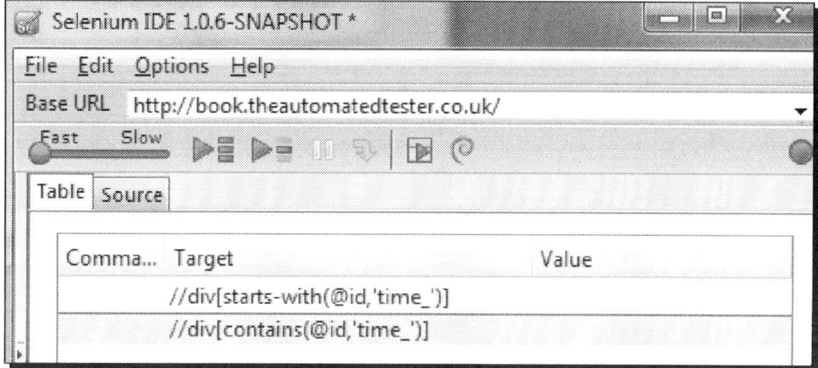

Finding an element by the text it contains

Finding elements by the text they contain can be quite useful when working with web pages that have been created dynamically. The elements could be from using a web-based WYSIWYG editor or you might just like to find a paragraph on the page with specific text to then do further queries on.

To do this, your query will need to have the `text()` method call in the query. It will match the entire contents of the node if it has the format `//element[text()='inner text']`. As seen in the previous section, your query can use the `contains` keyword to allow it to have a bit more leniency towards what it finds. The next screenshot displays a collection of queries that will find the same element as the previous section:

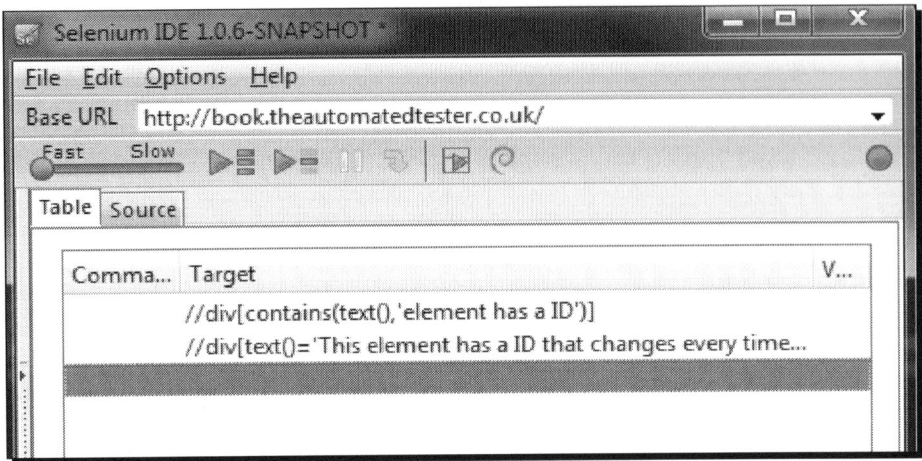

Using XPath axis to find elements

As we have seen, XPath is normally only used if the element we need to interact with is not accessible by normal means. In this section of the chapter, we are going to have a look at leveraging XPath axis in our queries to find the element that we wish to interact with.

An example that I have used in the real world was to find a table cell that had specific text and then traverse the tree backwards to find the edit button so that I could click on it. This may seem like an extreme example just to click on an edit button, but it is extremely common according to the Selenium Users forum on Google Groups.

In the first example, we are going to find a button and then find its sibling. In this example, the query that we will generate is equivalent to `xpath=//div[@class='leftdiv']/input[2]`. We will start by finding the first element for our query, which is `//input[@value='Button with ID']`. Place that into the Selenium IDE **Target** box and see which element it highlights. There is another button below the one that is highlighted, and that is the element that we need to work with in this section. The button is the next input item in the HTML, so it is elements `following-sibling` that we need. Our locator will look like `//input[@value='Button with ID']/following-sibling::input[@value='Sibling Button']`, and if it was placed into the Selenium IDE, it would be able to find the element that we are after, as seen in the next screenshot:

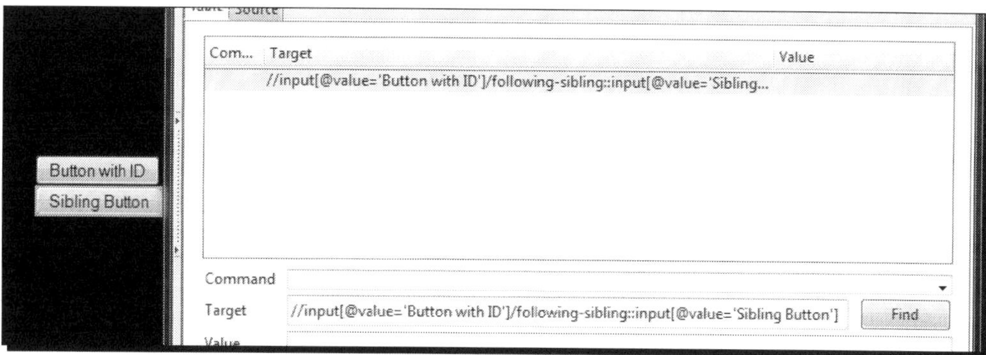

As mentioned earlier, you can use XPath to find an element and then walk backwards up the tree. If we were to take the example that we have just done and reverse it, you will need to start at the button with the value **Sibling Button** and then go back to the button with the value **Button with ID**.

We can see it finding the element in the next screenshot:

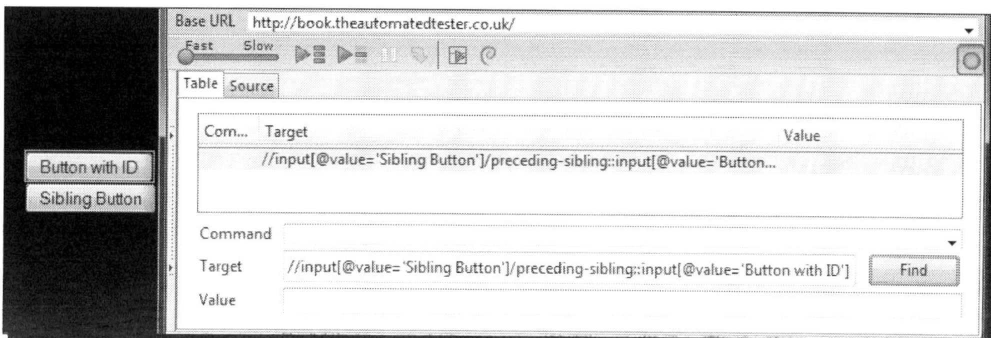

The next table contains a list of axes that you can use in your XPath queries to find the elements on the page:

Axis name	Result
ancestor	Selects all the ancestors (parent, grandparent, and so on) of the element
descendant	Selects all the descendants (children, grandchildren, and so on) of the element
following	Selects all elements that follow the closing tab of the current element
following-sibling	Selects all the siblings after the current element
parent	Selects the parent of the current element
preceding	Selects all elements that are before the current element
preceding-sibling	Selects all of the siblings before the current element

> As we have seen, there are a number of different ways to find the same element on the web page. However, having XPath queries in your test can be really useful for finding elements on the page but can slow down your test. Browsers such as Internet Explorer 6 do not have built-in XPath libraries and rely on doing the XPath query through JavaScript, which can mean that a test using XPath can run two or more times slower than a test with IDs. The more complex the XPath the slower the test because it needs to do more DOM traversals, which is an expensive operation.
>
> There is also another way to do XPath-like queries against the DOM and use built-in libraries in most browsers. We can use CSS selectors, which is the next section of this book.

Pop quiz – using XPath axis

- If you wanted do a partial match on an attribute on an element from the beginning of the value, which two of the following would you use:
  - `contains()`
  - `starts-with()`
  - `ends-with()`

Have a go hero

Go to `http://financial-dictionary.thefreedictionary.com/` and use `contains()`, `starts-with()`, and `ends-with()` on the page. Use the call `getXPathCount()` to see how many items you can get with your XPath query.

CSS selectors

We saw in the previous section that XPath selectors can offer your tests a lot of flexibility to find elements on the page.

Time for action – finding elements by CSS

So finding Elements by XPath can be an extremely costly exercise. A way around this is to use CSS selectors to find the objects that you need. Selenium is compatible with CSS 1.0, CSS 2.0, and CSS 3.0 selectors. There are a number of items that are supported such as namespace in CSS 3.0 and some pseudo classes and pseudo elements.

The syntax of your locator will look like `css=cssSelector`. Let's create our first selector to find an element on our page.

1. Open the Selenium IDE.
2. Open Firebug and click on the **Firefinder** tab.
3. We are going to look at one of the buttons in the div with the ID `divontheleft`. The CSS Selector for the buttons would be `div.leftdiv input`. Place that into **Firefinder** and click on the **Filter** button.
4. Your browser should show something like the next screenshot:

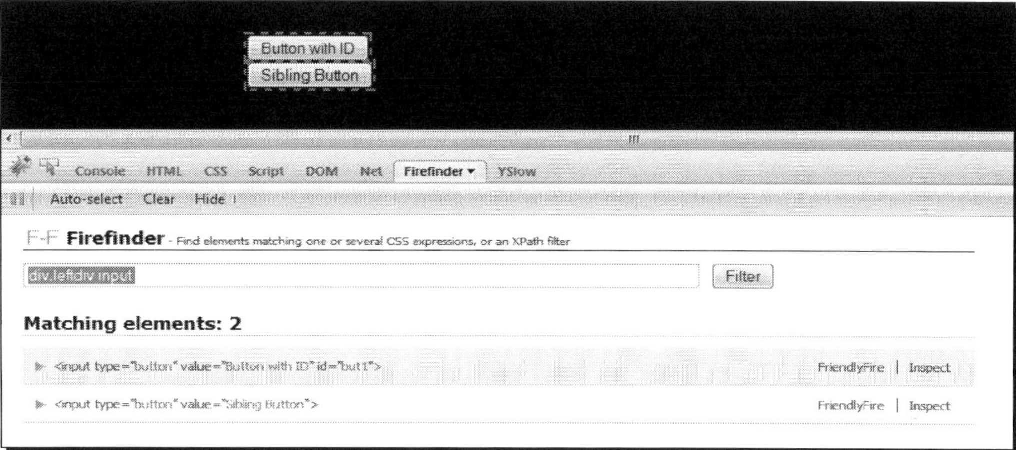

5. If you were now to put this into the Selenium IDE as `css=div.leftdiv input` and click on the **Find** button, it should look like the next screenshot:

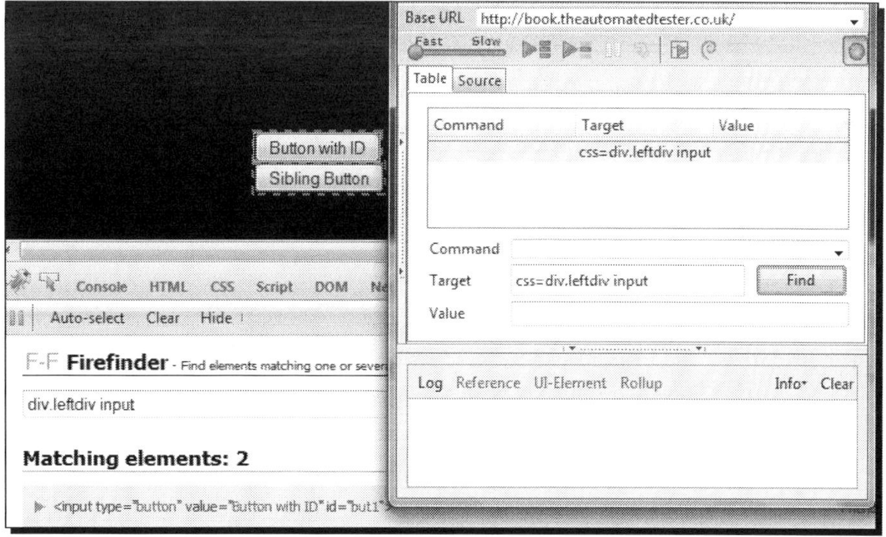

What just happened?

We have seen how Selenium has used the same CSS selector to find a button. Unlike in normal CSS, Selenium is only interested in the first element that matches the query and that is why in the second picture only the first button was highlighted and not its sibling.

Using child nodes to find the element

In the previous example, we saw that we were able to find the input button that was a child of the div node in the DOM. `div.leftdiv input` will look for the div and then look for an input node in the DOM, which is below that. It looks for any descendent that will match. This is the equivalent to using `descendent` in your XPath query.

If we needed to look for the child of the element, we would have to place `>` between the div selector and the input selector. Your locator would look like `css=div.leftdiv > input`. In the case of the `chapter2` page of the website, both will work, as they are direct children of `div.leftdiv`.

Using sibling nodes to find the element

Finding elements by using a sibling node in the DOM is probably the most common way to access an element. In the XPath section of this chapter, we saw that we could use the `following-sibling` operator in the XPath query. The equivalent CSS selector syntax is a `+` between DOM nodes in the query. It will check its direct next node to see if it matches, until it finds the element. So working against the HTML given next, we will create a CSS selector to find the second input button.

```
<div id="divontheleft" class="leftdiv">
  <input id='but1' value='Button with ID' type='button'/>
  <br/>
  <input value='Sibling Button' type='button'/>
</div>
```

`css=input#but1` will find the first button, and then its sibling is the `br`, and its sibling is `input`. The final selector will look like this: `css=input#but1 + br + input`. You can see this in the Selenium IDE in the next screenshot:

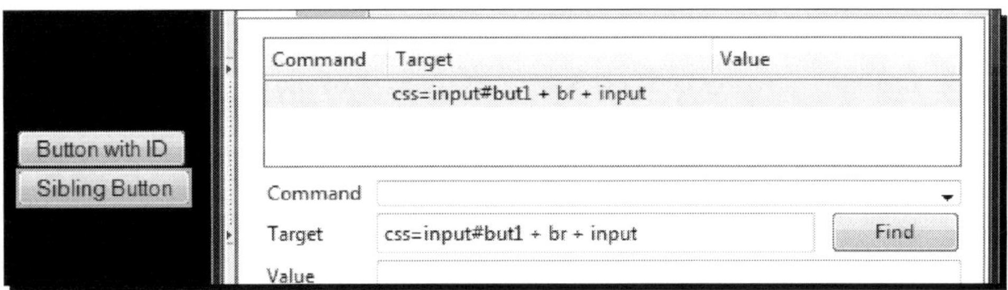

Using CSS class attributes in CSS selectors

Finding elements by their CSS class is going to be the most common method. A lot of the queries that people create start with a containing node distinguishing it by the CSS class and then moving through the DOM to a child or grandchild node to find the element that you wish to work again. The syntax for finding the item is to put the node such as a div, then put a full stop, and then the class. For example, to find the div with the class `centerdiv`, it would look like `css=div.centerdiv`.

Using element IDs in CSS selectors

As we saw in XPath queries, there are times we need to find the element that is next to an element that's a known ID. This means that we can access a lot more of the DOM, and because it is a CSS selector, there is a good chance that it will be a lot faster than its XPath equivalent.

To find an element by ID in a CSS selector, we need to place a # in front of the ID of the element in the CSS selector. For example, if we wanted to find a `div` with the ID of `divinthecenter`, the CSS selector would look like this: `css=div#divinthecenter`.

If you were to place this in the **Target** textbox of the Selenium IDE and click on **Find**, it should highlight the item, as seen in the next screenshot:

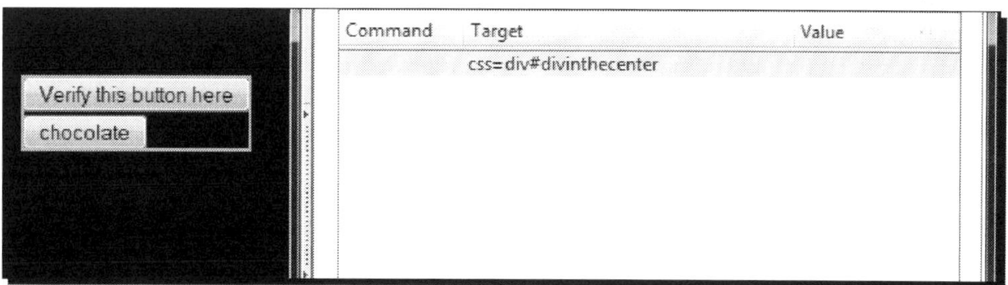

Finding elements by their attributes

In the XPath queries section, we saw how useful it could be to find an element by looking at its attributes. It could be that an element may have the same name but a different value, so finding them according to their attributes can be extremely powerful. In this example, we are going to look for the button that has the value **chocolate**. On web page buttons, it's the value that is displayed on the screen.

The syntax for looking at the attribute is `node[attribute='value']`. So in the case of the button with the value **chocolate**, it will be `input[value='chocolate']`. If you were to put that into the Selenium IDE, it will have the format `css=input[value='chocolate']`, and when you click on the **Find** button, you will see the following:

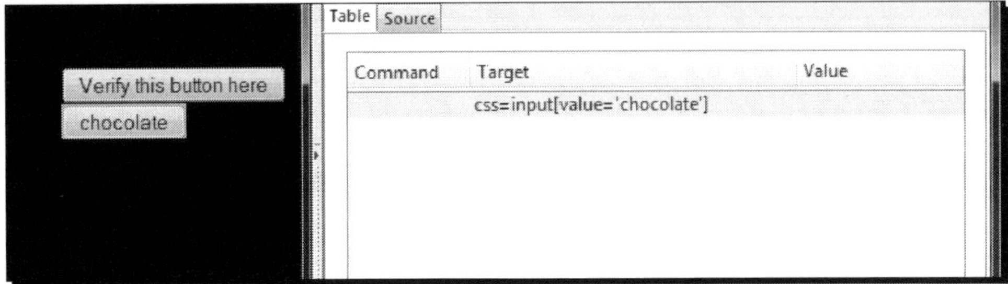

Another example of this is if you were trying to find an element according to its `href`. The syntax for that would be `a[href='path']`. You can try this on the `index` page and try to find the link to this chapter. When you have done it, it should look something like `css=a[href='/chapter2']`. If you click on the **Find** button, it will highlight the `chapter 2` link.

Chaining of attributes is also supported in Selenium to make sure that your test is using one specific element on the page. The syntax will be `css=node[attr1='value1'][attr2='value2']`. An example on the page that we are working against would be `css=input[id='but1'][value='Button with ID']`. This will find the button with the value **Button with ID**. You can chain as many attributes as you want in this manner.

Partial matches on attributes

In XPath queries we saw that we could use `contains` to find partial matches of values to attributes. This can be extremely useful for locating elements based on a part of their ID if it is dynamically generated. The next table explains the different syntax needed, and after that we have a look at some working examples.

Syntax	Description
`^=`	Finds the item starting with the value passed in. This is the equivalent to the XPath `starts-with`.
`$=`	Finds the item ending with the value passed in. This is the equivalent to the XPath `ends-with`.
`*=`	Finds the item that matches the attribute, which has the value that partially matches. This is equivalent to XPath `contains`.

In the XPath section of this chapter, we had a look at the XPath `//div[contains(@id,'time_')]`, which has a dynamic ID. The equivalent CSS selector would be `div[id^='time_']` or `div[id*='time_']`. The next screenshot shows both of the selectors highlighting the element that we want.

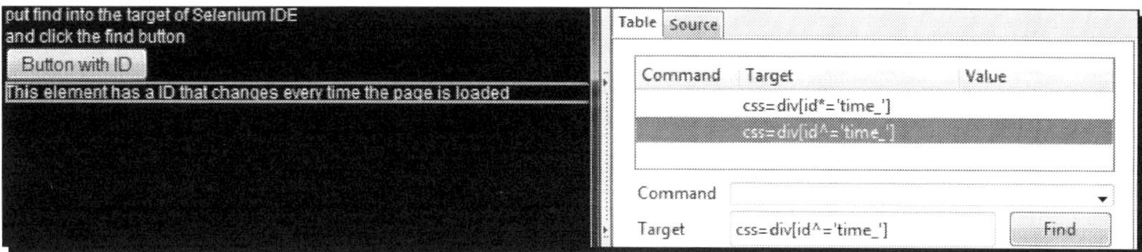

Finding the nth element with CSS

There are times where we need to find the nth element after a parent element on the page. In the XPath examples, we looked at the second input after the div with the class `leftdiv`. The `xpath` looked like: `xpath=//div[@class='leftdiv']/input[2]`. To find the second to nth element, we will need to use pseudo classes. Pseudo classes are used to add special effects to selectors. In this case, we are going to use `nth-child` for the first example.

1. Open the Selenium IDE.
2. Enter `css=div#divinthecenter *:nth-child(2)`. This will find the same as `xpath=//div[@class='leftdiv']/input[2]`.

3. Click on the **Find** button.

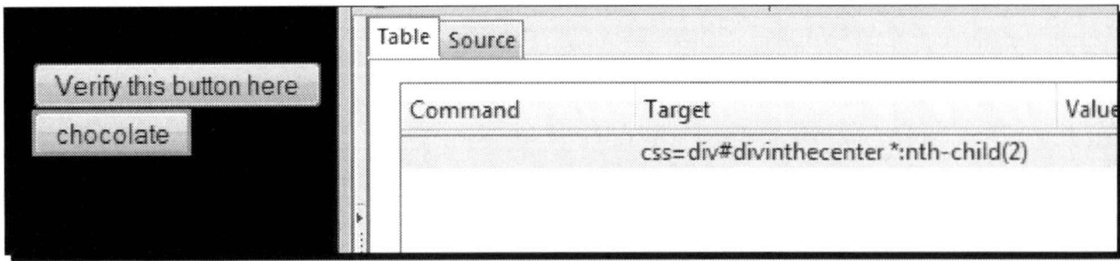

Unfortunately, Selenium does not support the `nth-of-type` pseudo class, so you will not be able to access the specific type. This is why the selector is using the wildcard `*` and then finding the `nth-child` from our starting div. The downside to using a selector in this manner is if any other node was placed in the way, it would make the tests fail.

Finding an element by its inner text

Finding elements by their inner text can also be quite useful. In the XPath section of this chapter we used the `text()` function to see the text it had. Earlier we had `xpath=//div[contains(text(),'element has a ID')]` to find a div with text in it. To update this XPath to a CSS selector we would need to use the `contains` pseudo class. The updated locator for CSS would be `css=div:contains('element has a ID')`. One important note on CSS selector is that it is not as granular as the XPath version because it may look at the descendants for the text.

It is important to know that CSS selectors only have a read forward process. This means that you cannot find an element and then traverse backwards up the DOM. This is what makes CSS selectors a lot faster than XPath queries to find the same elements.

Pop quiz – using locators

- What is the most common way to find an element on a page?
    - ID
    - XPath
    - CSS selector
    - Name

- If you wanted to find the sibling input that is after an input in the DOM, what would the XPath look like?
- What would the CSS look like for the previous question?

Have a go hero – working against Google Maps

Now that you have managed to create tests with different locators try working against Google Maps. It is an extremely good site to work with XPath and CSS, as it never has IDs or names.

Summary

We learned a lot in this chapter about locators. We have been able to use a large number of different methods to find the elements that are on a page. We have seen how to find elements using the easy methods such as `id=` and `name=` and doing queries against the DOM to find them using CSS selectors or XPath queries.

Specifically, we covered:

- **Using Firebug to find the element attributes**: In this section, we were able to start using Firebug. This will become an invaluable tool for anyone that works with web applications. It has a very good mechanism for finding elements, so you can work against them.
- **Finding an element by ID**: Elements can easily be found by the value of the ID attribute. This is the most common way to find elements and is the fastest way to find the elements on the page.
- **Finding an element by name**: When elements do not have the IDs but do have a name attribute, your tests can use those.
- **Finding an element by DOM query**: In this section, we were able to use the power of JavaScript DOM API calls to find the element that we wish to work with. This can be from the most basic call to the document to a JavaScript function that you can pass variables to.
- **Finding an element using XPath queries**: In this section, we were able to find the element on the page by using XPath queries. Your test can use relative paths or even XPath functions to find the element on the page. The queries can be as complex as you want, but remember that they can impact the speed of the test.
- **Finding an element using CSS selectors**: When your XPath queries are making your tests run slow, especially in browsers that do not have good support for XPath, CSS selectors are starting to become the default way to find elements on web pages with popular JavaScript libraries and it is not a large learning curve to get working with it.

We also discussed how XPath queries can make tests run slower on browsers that do not have native XPath support. Internet Explorer 6 is the main browser where you would see this issue. When tests start running extremely slowly with XPath, we can move our tests over to CSS to see large speed gains in our tests.

If locator does not have the locator type identifier in front of it, Selenium will default to the following strategies:

- **DOM**: For locators starting with `document`
- **XPath**: For locators starting with `//`
- **Identifier**: For any other locator

Now that we've learned how to locate the elements on the page, we're ready to see how we can use regular expressions in our tests—which is the topic of the next chapter.

3
Pattern Matching

In this chapter, we are going to discuss how to harness the powers of regular expressions and globs to verify that text on the page matches our pattern. This is going to be used extensively in the way we verify or assert that items are on the page. This can either be checking that the exact text is on the page, checking that it is a partial match or checking that it matches a regular expression. These make our tests very powerful.

In this chapter, we shall:

- Make sure text is exact in elements
- Use globs to verify text
- Use regular expressions

So let's get on with it...

Verifying exact text

In this section of the chapter, we are going to have a look at verifying that the exact text is in an element. This can be used to check that the relevant items are being populated in a table or to check that a div used to store the username is actually storing it.

This is done by using a special prefix `exact:` in front of the item. Let's see how to use this with our first *Time for action*.

Time for action – verifying text

Let's say that you have a web application that generates pages dynamically according to the path. In this example, we are going to use the `exact:` prefix to check that the exact text is in the element on the page.

1. Navigate to `http://book.theautomatedtester.co.uk/chapter3/yourname` where `yourname` in the URL has been replaced.
2. Verify that the div with the ID `name` contains your name exactly.
3. Run your test.

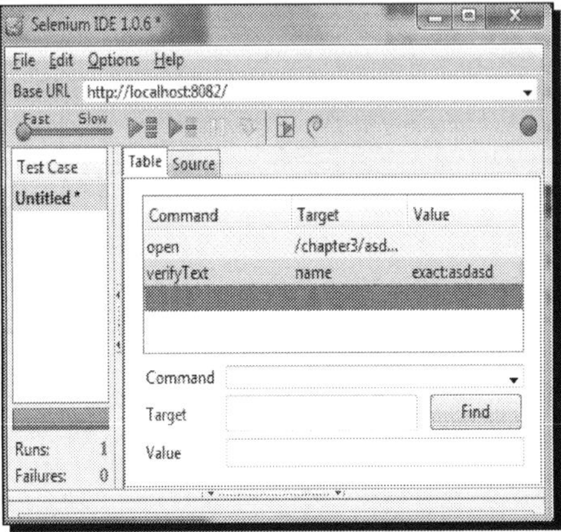

What just happened?

We have seen that we can check for the exact text on the page.

If we were to make a change, say, removing a character from the value we were expecting, it would fail the test as you can see in the next screenshot:

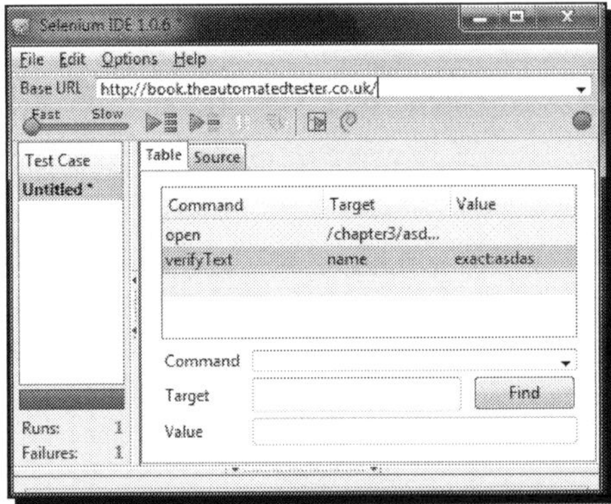

Using the `exact:` prefix means that if the capitalization of an item is not correct, the test will fail. We can see how this fails in the next screenshot:

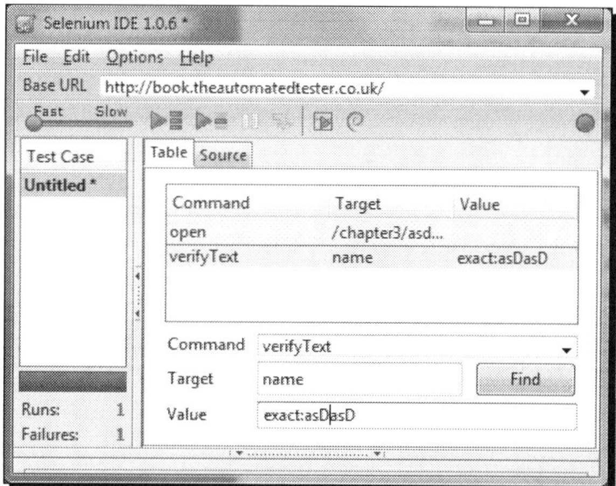

Time for action – using exact: on links

You can also use this on links, as we can see in our next *Time for action*. This means that we can make sure the test always clicks on the correct link.

1. Open `http://book.theautomatedtester.co.uk/chapter3/yourname` where `yourname` is your name.
2. Click on the link `Index`, but make sure you add the `exact:` prefix.
3. Run your test. It should look similar to the next screenshot:

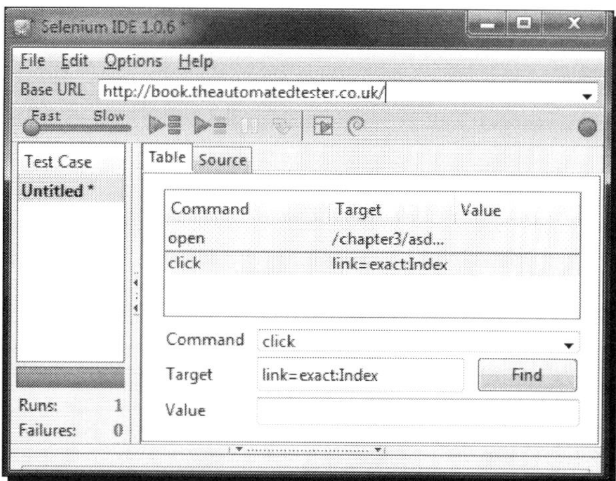

What just happened?

As we just saw, we can use the `exact:` prefix on links to make sure that only the links that match the text exactly are clicked. This is a good way to make sure that the link exists and to click on it without the need to have a verify command before the click.

Pop quiz – using exact: in locators

- Does `exact:` allows capitalization differences?
  - ❑ True
  - ❑ False
- Does `exact:` only work on text in links?

Have a go hero – using exact: in locators

Go to your favorite site and do a number of verifies and asserts on the page as well as clicking on different links. Make sure that you try your test with different capitalization. Don't worry if you can't get it to work on everything at first because we will try different techniques throughout this chapter.

Using globs in our tests

In the previous section of this chapter, we learned how we can harness exact matches in our tests. However, this can be a little frustrating when you want to test something in a div but the surrounding text might change suddenly. There is a technique called globbing. It is similar to regular expressions, but is quite limited in its syntax.

Globs are used extensively throughout Selenium as the default pattern matching technique. Most users are normally looking for part of a sentence when verifying or asserting in their tests.

We can now have a go at creating our first test with a glob.

Time for action – using globs in tests

Let's say that we have a web application that shows us what a user's star sign is and what the current date is. For a test the only thing that people would be concerned with is if it returns the correct star sign. A good example of this is the `verifyTextPresent` call, which will apply the glob to the entire page.

1. Open up the Selenium IDE.

2. Navigate to `http://book.theautomatedtester.co.uk/chapter3`.
3. Using `verifyTextPresent` check that the star sign Virgo is on the page.
4. Run your test.

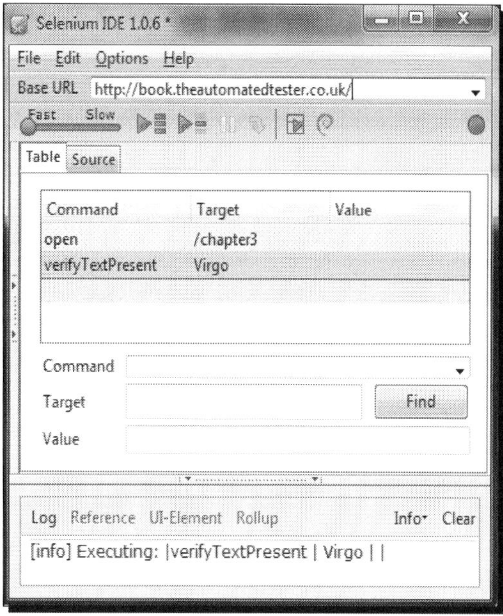

What just happened?

We have created a test that verifies that a specific string can be found in the HTML page. This is useful for making sure that an element is in the page, no matter where it is located on the page. This could be something like the terms or privacy statements. As with most commands in Selenium, there is an inverse version called `verifyTextNotPresent` for when you want to check that a certain string is not found on the page.

As mentioned earlier, globs have a regular expression like syntax. If you wanted to check that a string text on the page had the letters "cap" on it and did not care about the rest of the characters that may follow, the syntax for that would be `cap*`. This is telling Selenium to find anything with the name "cap" and any letters that follow it. This is similar to the way a command prompt handles it. It is an extremely greedy way to find a match, as it will look at anything that looks vaguely correct.

Let's see this in action.

Time for action – using * to find a basic pattern

Let's say that we have a website that is used as a dictionary and we wanted to validate that on the "CA" pages of the dictionary where there was "cap" and any other letters that follow. Or similarly you wanted to check that there are strings that start with "b" and end with "k". In the next example, we are going to see how we can verify these patterns.

1. Open up the Selenium IDE.
2. Navigate to `http://book.theautomatedtester.co.uk/chapter3`.
3. Note `verifyText` under the **UI-Element**, `divinthecenter` has `*Cap*`.
4. Run your test, and it should look similar to the next screenshot.

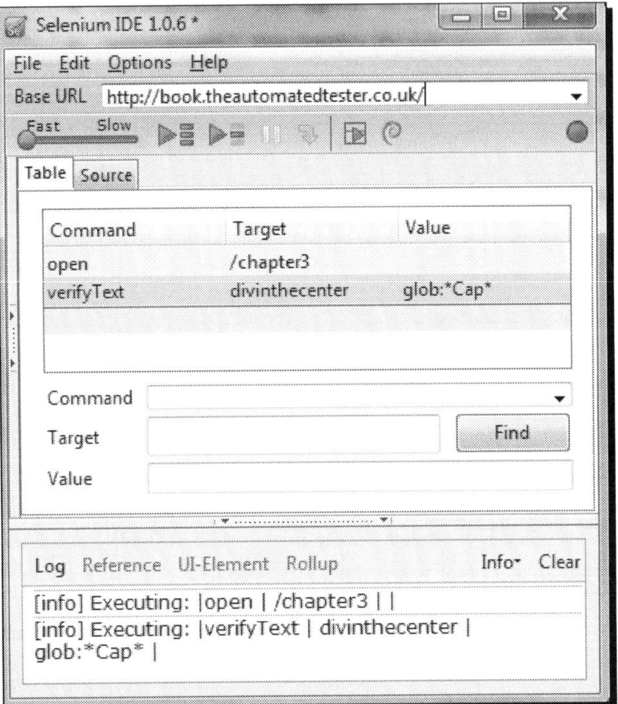

What just happened?

We have just run a test that uses the glob wildcard pattern matching. This is useful if you just want to check that text strings on the page match a very basic pattern. The `*` will match anything that follows. So in the previous example, when we wanted to find if there was text with `Cap` on the page, we put a `*` at the start and end of the pattern.

There are times when we just want to make sure that it checks for one character difference. We do this by using `?` in our pattern matching. For example, to check that a pattern is four characters long and the last three characters are `ool`, for `pool` or `cool`, we would use the `?` at the beginning so that the pattern that we match is `?ool`.

Let's see this in action.

Time for action – using ? in a glob pattern

As mentioned before, it might be good to check that there is one character difference in your test. In this *Time for action*, we are going to check that we have a word ending in '`ool`' in the div `leftdiv`.

1. Open up the Selenium IDE.
2. Navigate to `http://book.theautomatedtester.co.uk/chapter3`.
3. Note that `verifyText` in `leftdiv` matches `?ool`.
4. Run your test and it should look similar to the next screenshot:

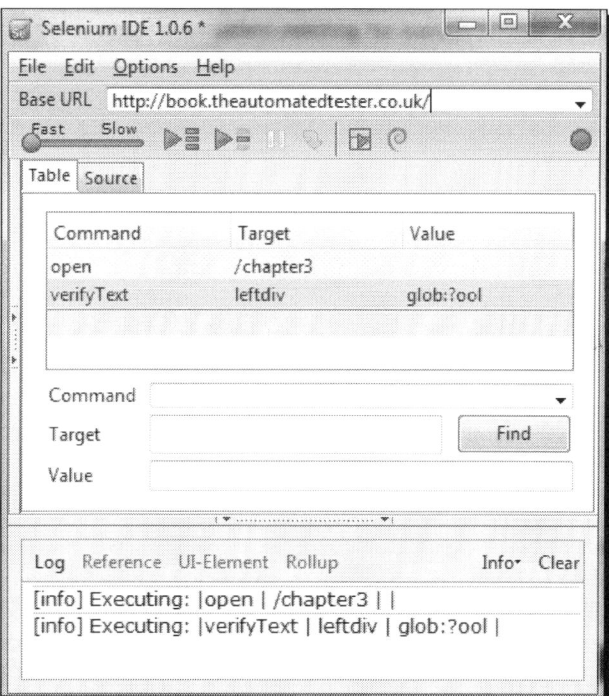

What just happened?

We have just checked that `sometext` on the page ended with `ool`. The page will randomly pick a word and then render it on the page, so hardcoding the value in the test will make the test fail when it should not.

We can also use character classes as part of our globbing.

Time for action – using character classes in globbing

We have seen how we can use an all-capturing syntax for globbing with `*`. There are times where we would only want it to be in a group of letters: for example, if we knew that it was going to be in the group of c, f, p, m, and we only wanted to accept that we would need to do `glob:[cfmp]ool`.

Let's see this in action.

1. Open the Selenium IDE.
2. Navigate to `http://book.theautomatedtester.co.uk/chapter3`.
3. Verify that text is present using the `glob:[cfmp]ool`.
4. Run your test.

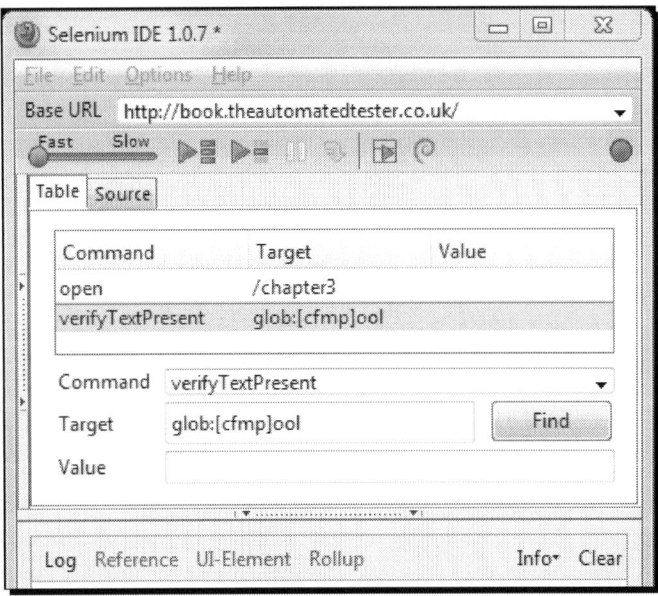

What just happened?

We have just seen how we can use character classes as part of our globbing pattern matching to verify or assert that text is on the page. This can be quite useful if you don't care about the exact text that will appear on the screen, but you want to make sure that it conforms to a basic pattern.

Pop quiz – using globbing

- What will the `*` item in a glob pattern do for `goog*`?
- What will the `?` item do in the glob pattern `?ool`?

Have a go hero – using globbing

Now that you have confidence in using globbing have a go at creating new tests using this new found knowledge. Go to your favorite blog and try to use globbing patterns.

You can use `*` `?` and character classes.

Using regular expressions

Globbing patterns are useful, but they do not give us a way to check that a field has numbers. They also prevents us from ignoring capitalization. For all of these cases, we can start to use regular expressions. Regular expressions are used extensively throughout applications from input validation to text manipulation. We tell Selenium to use regular expressions by putting `regexp:` in front of a string we want to check.

Let's see this in action.

Time for action – using basic regular expressions to check the date

In this section, we are going to check that the date on the page follows the pattern of three letters for the day, two numbers for the day of the month, three letters for the month, and four numbers for the year. The regular expression for this would be `\w{3} \d{2} \w{3} \d{4}`. The `\w` will look for word characters and `\d` will look for digit characters and the figure in between `{}` tells the expression how many times it should expect each type.

Now let's do this in Selenium

1. Open up the Selenium IDE.
2. Navigate to `http://book.theautomatedtester.co.uk/chapter3`.
3. Note `verifyText` in the div with the ID `centerdiv` with the **Value** field populated `regexp:\w{3} \d{2} \w{3} \d{4}`.
4. Run the test and it should look similar to the next screenshot.

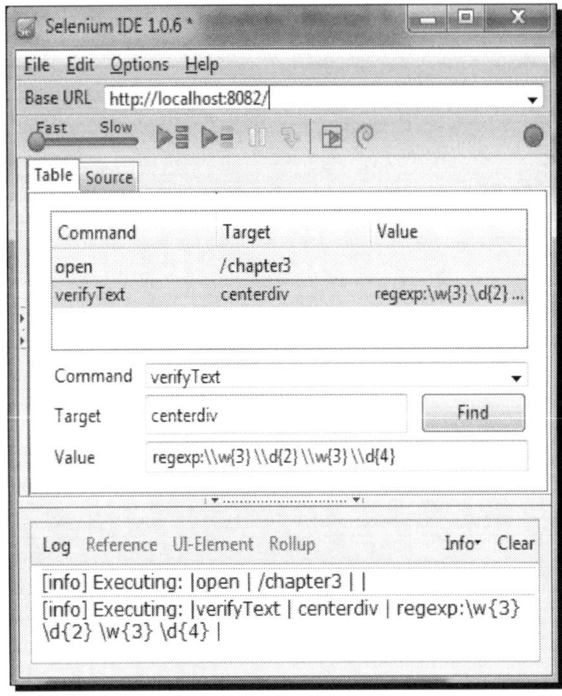

What just happened?

We just had a look at creating a test with a regular expression. This is quite useful for checking that there is a date on the page and that it conforms to a certain pattern. This is useful for checking dates that are not the day of the test. We had a look at how we can check for letters and digits on the page.

Sometimes we do not know how many characters are going to be in the area, but we do know it has letters or numbers. This means that we cannot use globbing to check but we can use a greedy query nearly the same as globbing in our regular expression.

Time for action – using regular expression wildcards

To use wildcards, we can use the . (dot) operator followed by either a * or a +. The * tells the regular expression that there will be instances between "0" and "n", while the + tells the regular expression that there will be instances between "1" and "n". Let's see this in a test.

1. Open the Selenium IDE.
2. Navigate to `http://book.theautomatedtester.co.uk/chapter3/yourname` where yourname is replaced by your name.
3. Note `verifyText` in the div with the ID `name`. Match either letters or numbers and add the wildcard such as `\d.*`.
4. Run the test and it should look similar to the next screenshot:

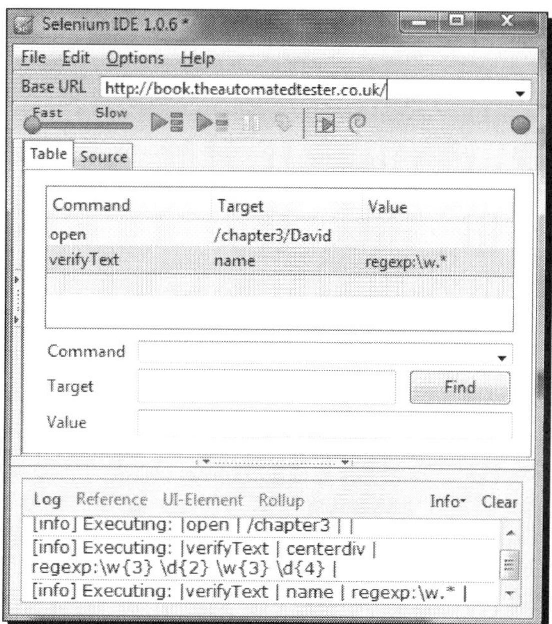

What just happened?

We have just applied wildcards to our tests. This can be useful if we do not know how long the text is going to be, or if we don't need to know what appears in the centre of a string.

There are times that we do care what the complete string could be and then we apply matches for letters. We do this by using `[a-z]` or any other similar regular expression operators.

Pop quiz – using regular expressions

- What is the best way to check if a word is three characters long?
- What is the way to add wild cards to a regular expression?

Have a go hero – using regular expressions

Now that we have a good understanding of how regular expressions work, let us try to create a few more tests with regular expressions. Write tests to work against your favorite blog. Make sure that there are sentences that match a certain length.

Use the `\w` and `\s` `regex` syntax.

Summary

We learned a lot in this chapter about pattern matching. We saw how we can make sure that the areas match the text we want exactly by using the prefix `exact:` or by using globbing like we do in command prompts. We then moved onto harnessing regular expressions for those moments where globbing doesn't have the power we need.

Specifically, we covered the following topics:

- **Using exact pattern matching**: We saw that by prefixing our search string with `exact:` we could make sure that elements match exactly to what we are expecting.
- **Using globbing patterns**: Sometimes we need to use basic patterns to make sure text on the page matches what we are expecting. Globbing is used in command prompts, so this section reinforced what you already knew.
- **Using regular expressions**: This section showed us how we can use regular expressions to find what we need on the page. It allows us to be more expressive as well as stricter with patterns when verifying or asserting text on the page.

Now that we've learned about pattern matching, we're ready to start having a look at using JavaScript in our test—which is the topic of the next chapter.

4
Using JavaScript

In this chapter, we are going to have a look at using JavaScript in our tests. JavaScript is the base language of Selenium, so it can handle modifications. If you need to manipulate a web page during the test, there are a number of different calls that one could use. This means that if Selenium cannot offer you all the functionality either through calls or needing to call other JavaScript functions, you can use JavaScript within your Selenium script. This is so that we can test some of the hard-to-test scenarios that we will one day come across.

In this chapter, we shall cover topics such as:

- Using JavaScript
- Using variables in your tests with JavaScript
- Accessing the browser with JavaScript
- Firing events on elements

So let's get on with it...

Using JavaScript as our test language

JavaScript is a very flexible language and has had the title of language for the Web for a while. We can see it being used every day to make web applications look and feel like desktop applications thanks to AJAX.

Using the same language in our tests is quite useful because, as previously mentioned, JavaScript is the main underlying language of Selenium. In this section of the chapter, we are going to have a look at how we can use JavaScript in our tests. This can be for creating unique items that are needed for the test or if you wanted to enter today's date in your test.

To specify that something is going to contain JavaScript, you will need to put `javascript{ }` into the target or value box within the Selenium IDE. You will need to place your JavaScript statement within the { } in `javascript{ }`. When passing JavaScript into Selenium, it is evaluated and the last statement in the JavaScript will return into your test. An example of this would be:

```
var a, b;
a = 2;
b = 5;
a+b;
```

This sample would return `7` to Selenium so that it can be used later.

Let's see this in action now.

Time for action – using JavaScript to enter text into a field

Imagine that you are testing a web application that requires you to type today's date into a textbox. Let's see how one would do that.

1. Open the Selenium IDE.
2. Navigate to `http://book.theautomatedtester.co.uk/chapter4`.
3. Use the `type` command on the locator `dateInput` to put in the result of the following JavaScript: `javascript{ Date() }`.
4. Run your script. It should look similar to the next screenshot.

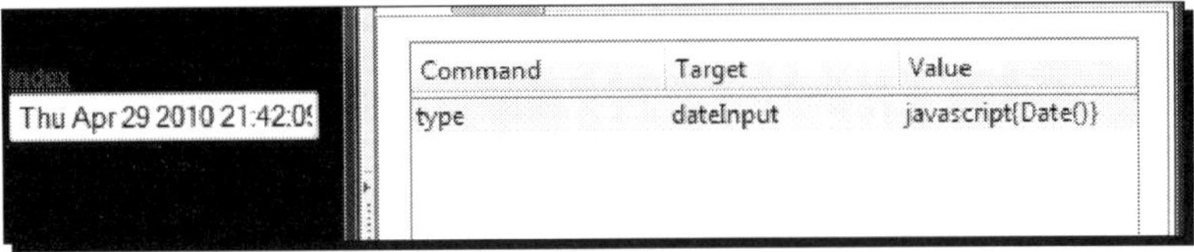

What just happened?

As you can see from the screenshot, the command we used has typed something into the textbox. In this case, we just had one `javascript` statement, which was `javascript{Date()}`, and that was placed into the input box.

Let's now have a look at using multiple statements to calculate the current hour of the day.

Time for action – using multiple statements in your JavaScript

Imagine that you need to type the current hour into your tests. Your test will need to get the current date and time and then use the JavaScript `Date` object to return the current hour.

1. Open the Selenium IDE.
2. Navigate to `http://book.theautomatedtester.co.uk/chapter4`.
3. In the same box as we used earlier, type the current hour. The JavaScript is `javascript{ d = new Date();d.getHours()}`.
4. Run your script. It will look similar to the next screenshot.

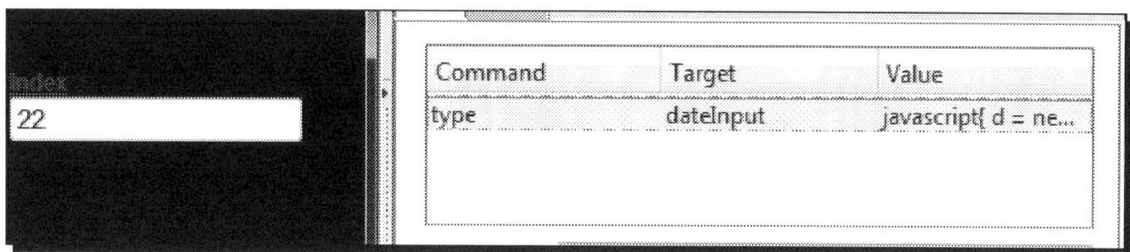

What just happened?

We have now had our test use multiple statements in the test. The `javascript` you will have created will look something like `javascript{ d = new Date();d.getHours()}`. The `d.getHours()` call will return the current hour to Selenium and that is what will be typed.

Now that we have the confidence to start using JavaScript in our tests, we can have a look at storing the value from `javascript` in our tests to be used in multiple places. The store command takes values either from JavaScript snippets or from elements on the page so that we can reuse them later.

Time for action – storing the result of JavaScript in a variable

Imagine that you are writing a test for a hotel booking: you need to calculate a date in a week's time, and then on a different page, you needed to verify that it was there. You would then use the `storeEval` command to store the result and then use it again as we did in Chapter 1, *Getting Started with Selenium IDE*. Let's try this in the Selenium IDE.

1. Open the Selenium IDE.
2. Create a step to `storeEval` with the JavaScript, `javascript{ 10 * 10 }`, and use the variable `hundred`.

3. Using the `echo` command, show the result.

4. Run the script. It should look similar to the next screenshot.

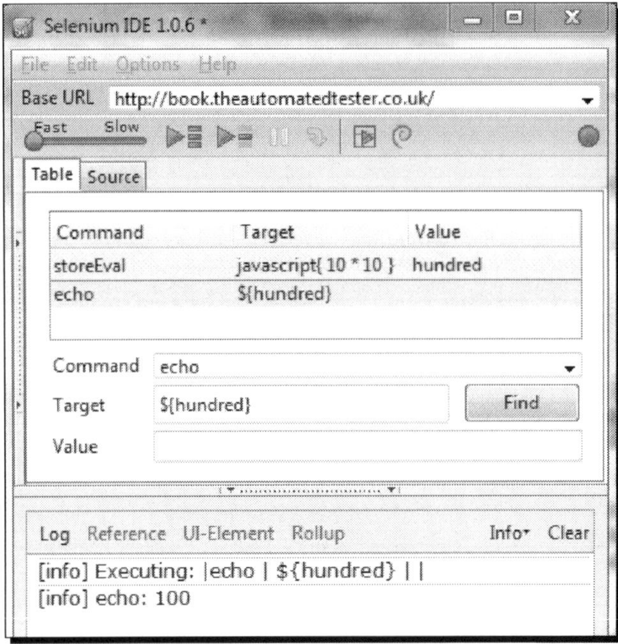

What just happened?

We just saw how we can use Selenium to evaluate some JavaScript and store the result. This can be used in a number of different scenarios—from needing to store a date calculated in a booking system to generating a unique ID for a registration process. It allows the test to create test data and store it for later use either by typing it or by using it in an *assert* or *verify*.

Your tests will be able to take full advantage of JavaScript, so the tests do not have to use hardcoded values.

Pop quiz – using JavaScript

- What is the syntax to use `javascript` in a test?
  - `{ 1 + 1 }`
  - `JS { 1 + 1 }`
  - `javascript{ 1 + 1 }`
- In a multiline JavaScript statement, how do you return to Selenium?

Have a go hero – doing more with JavaScript

Create a script against your favourite calendar web application. Write some JavaScript to pick a date two weeks from the day the test is run. Your test will need to make sure that it handles dates where day is two digits and month is two digits.

Using Selenium variables with JavaScript

Now that we have a good understanding of how we can pass and evaluate JavaScript in our tests, let's start combining it with variables that we generated in our tests. These variables would have been created using one of the store commands, such as `storeText`.

There are a number of different scenarios that require a test to have this. Your application may be an auction site that requires you to store the text of the current highest bid, and then add something to that value to try moving the bidding to a higher value.

To do this we will need to make sure that our tests call the Selenium variable by accessing the `storedVars` dictionary. This is the object that is used in all store commands to store the result of that command. The variable that we use in the store command is the key for the dictionary. The results are stored in the value object of the key/value pair.

Now that we have the basic knowledge of how it works, let's see this in action.

Time for action – using Selenium variables with JavaScript

Let's imagine you are working against an auction site. The script will need to get the value of the last highest bid off the page and then add `2` to it. Let's try this in the Selenium IDE.

1. Open the Selenium IDE.
2. Navigate to `http://book.theautomatedtester.co.uk/chapter4`.
3. Create a step to store the text from the span with the ID `bid`.
4. Create a step to add `5` to the variable we used to store the result of the previous step.

5. Run your test. It should look similar to the next screenshot.

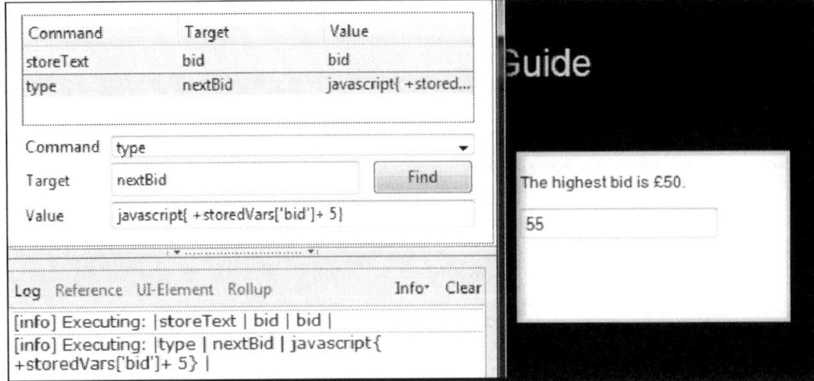

What just happened?

In this test, we have seen how we can get something off the page and store that in a variable. We then used this variable to add something to it. This was an example of a test for an auction site. The `storedVars` dictionary was called to get the value of the `bid` variable. `storedVars['bid']` is equivalent to `${bid}` that we would use if we were using a `type` command.

As a side note, the `+` in front of the `storedVars` is syntactic sugar to change it from a string to an integer. This is the same as doing `storedVars['bid']*1`.

Let's see how we can use this within a verify or assert.

Time for action – JavaScript within a verify or assert

Let's say that you have stored a value from a different part of the test and now you need to verify or assert that the value is correct.

1. Open the Selenium IDE.
2. Navigate to `http://book.theautomatedtester.co.uk/chapter4`.
3. Create a step to store the text in `bid`.
4. Create a step to verify that it is equal to `5*10` using the `verifyEval` command.
5. Run your test. It should look similar to the next screenshot.

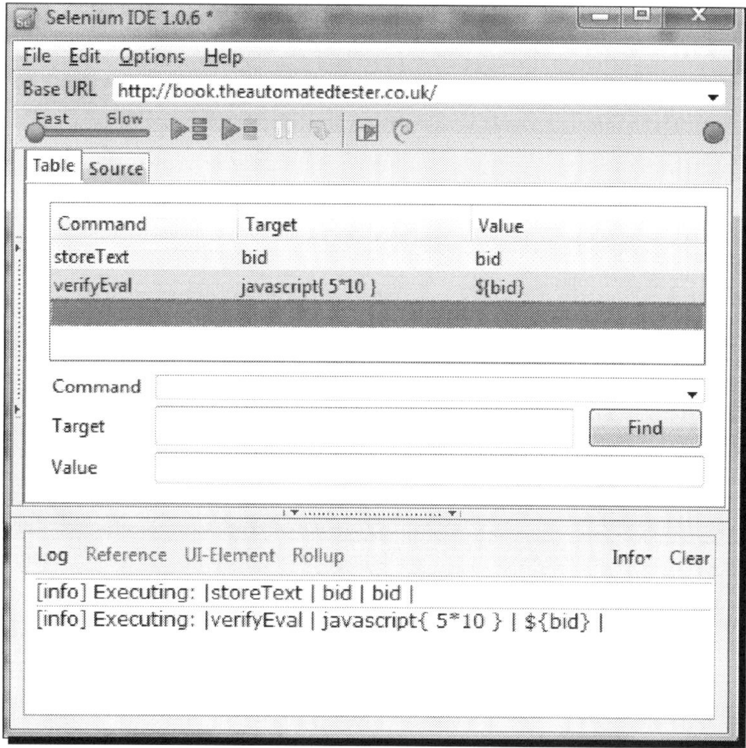

What just happened?

We have just created a test that uses a variable that we created, and then used it to verify that the JavaScript evaluated is the same. This can be useful in a number of different scenarios that the standard Selenium API can't help you with.

Pop quiz – using Selenium variables in JavaScript

- What is the variable that stores all the Selenium variables?

Have a go hero – using Selenium variables in JavaScript

Imagine that you are testing an online dictionary. You need to test how the phonetics are displayed so that people can work out how to pronounce the word. This means that you will need to store the word that it finds and then apply a basic algorithm to split the word into different parts.

Accessing the browser with JavaScript

There are times when it will be necessary to access the browser from within your tests. For instance, there may be a need to fire off a call to a JavaScript function on the page to check that it is doing what is expected. It could also be that you need to check that a certain condition has been met on the page so that your test can carry on.

Selenium is built from JavaScript so that it can interact with the page in the synthesized way that a user does. When doing this, Selenium wraps the DOM in a new object. This means that if you want to access the DOM in your test without using a specific Selenium command, you will need to access it through this special object. This object is called **browserbot** and it has access to the browser window. Your test will need to then call the window and you will have the `Window` object with which you can then do what you want. The syntax that you will need is:

```
var window = this.browserbot.getUserWindow();
```

BrowserBot

BrowserBot is the JavaScript object that allows Selenium to control the browser. It overrides access to the window, document, and other key browser JavaScript objects that we can normally access.

The call `getUserWindow()` returns the `Window` object. The call removes the `XPCNativeWrapper` that Firefox uses to wrap the `Window` object. The `XPCNativeWrapper` is a way to wrap up the `Window` object within Selenium that Firefox adds and only allows access to very basic DOM calls.

Now that we have a basic understanding of `browserbot`, let's see this in action.

Time for action – accessing the page with browserbot

Imagine that you need to call a JavaScript function on the page. This could be because you are working against elements that Selenium can't interact with and your test needs to call into the API to put something on the page. Or you might have to write some tests to exercise the JavaScript functions on the page.

Let's try and call the add JavaScript function and then work with the alert that appears.

1. Open the Selenium IDE.
2. Navigate to `http://book.theautomatedtester.co.uk/chapter4`.
3. Create a step to call the function `concatStrings` with two strings as parameters. I used "Selenium" and "IDE" in my call.

4. Verify the alert.

5. Run your script. It should look similar to the next screenshot.

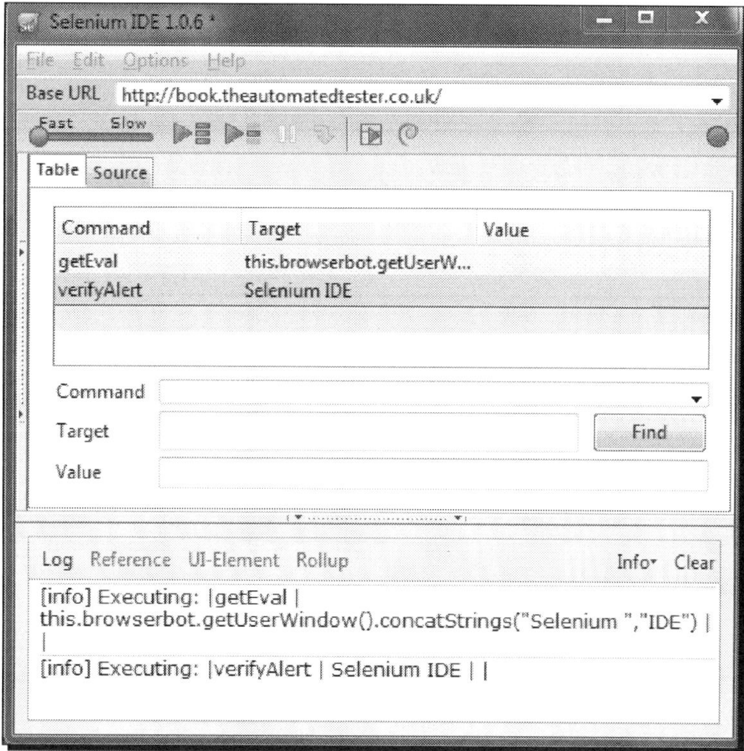

What just happened?

We have just had a test that calls into the page using JavaScript. This is useful when you want to check that a JavaScript API is returning what you expect, or if you need to access a JavaScript API to manipulate the page.

As we can see, this can be very useful for calling into a page to make something happen. However, what if you needed to test storing something on the page and then call the function?

There are times in a test when you will want to check the length of an internal array, or even check that there are a correct number of options within a `select` tag.

Let' see how we can do this.

Time for action – verifying a JavaScript evaluation with browserbot

Imagine that you need to check whether a select has a certain amount of options in it. This could be down to the fact that we don't know what order they are going to be in, so we cannot utilize a regular expression. Let's see how we can do this.

1. Open the Selenium IDE.
2. Navigate to `http://book.theautomatedtester.co.uk/chapter4`.
3. Create a step to verify that the select with the ID `selecttype` has four options in it.
4. Run your script. It should look similar to the next screenshot.

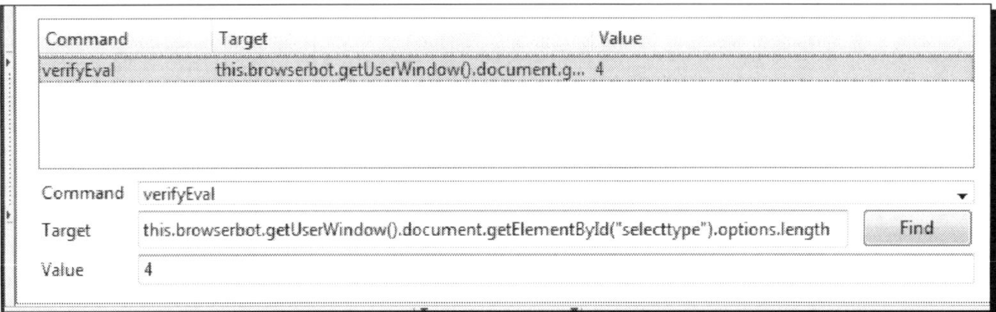

What just happened?

We have just seen how to verify that something on the page meets certain criteria. In this case, we wanted to check that the select with the ID `selecttype` had four options in it. This means our tests do not have to rely on Selenium commands. We can make small ad hoc calls in `javascript` to verify elements on the page.

There are times that you may want to do something similar but the options are loaded with AJAX. When that happens, we can then use the `waitForCondition`. This command will wait until it returns true. The call sits on the outside of the Selenium object, so if you work with it against the page, you will have to call into it. Instead of using `this.browserbot`, you will have to use `selenium.browserbot` in your JavaScript.

Let's see this in action.

Time for action – using waitForCondition

Let's imagine you have an application that has a `select` that is populated by AJAX. This is quite common for web applications that have `select`, which is populated by values within the database.

1. Open the Selenium IDE.
2. Navigate to `http://book.theautomatedtester.co.uk/chapter4`.
3. Create a step for `waitForCondition` to wait till the `select` is populated. There is an `options` property on the select that you can check the length of to see if it has loaded.
4. Run your script. It should look similar to the next screenshot.

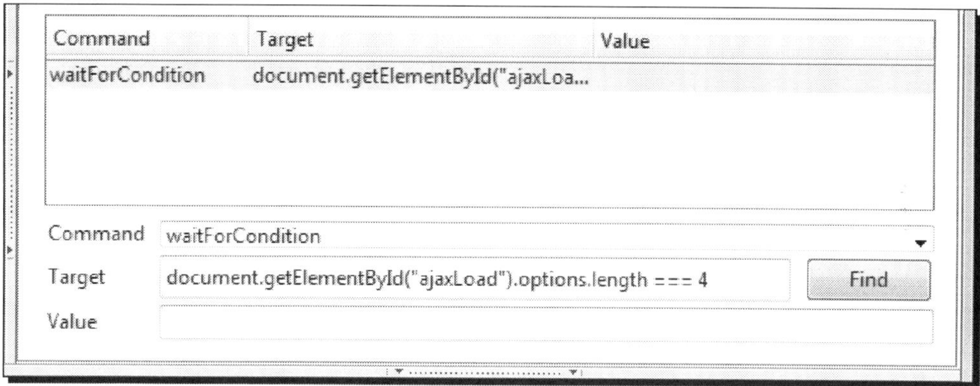

What just happened?

We just saw a command that had a look at the DOM. It then waited until a new item was loaded into the page. The `waitForCondition` command runs outside of Selenium. This is why in the previous example we explicitly called `selenium` instead of calling the parent with the `this` object.

Pop quiz – accessing the browser with JavaScript

- What is the object that allows our tests to access the page?
- Does `waitForCondition` sit inside or outside the `selenium` object?

Have a go hero – accessing the browser with JavaScript

Imagine that you are working against a WYSIWYG editor built into a page. Selenium cannot always type into `contentEditable` areas. A lot of common editor components have a way of programmatically accessing the `contentEditable` area. This means that you will need to use `storeEval` and other JavaScript calls to make this work.

Firing events

Sometimes there are situations where you may not be able to click on an element in the page. However, you need to make your test fire the click event. Selenium has an API call that allows us to fire the event that is attached to elements on a page.

```
<div id='fireEventDiv' onClick='alert("Alert Thrown")'>
```

The `fireEvent` call specifying `onClick` on the above `div` would cause the alert to be thrown. The `fireEvent` works against the following JavaScript events:

- `onFocus`
- `onBlur`
- `onChange`
- `onSubmit`
- `onMouseOut`
- `onMouseOver`

There are times where you might need to cause a `mouseOver` to fire off the JavaScript that is attached to that event.

Time for action – firing a mouseOver event

Imagine that you want to test a `mouseOver`, but the Selenium command `mouseOver` does not make your `mouseOver` fire. To get around this, your test will need to fire the event using the `fireEvent` command.

Let's see this in action:

1. Open the Selenium IDE.
2. Navigate to `http://book.theautomatedtester.co.uk/chapter4`.
3. Create a step with `fireEvent` against the element with the ID `hoverOver` for the event `mouseOver`.

4. Run your script. It should look similar to the next screenshot.

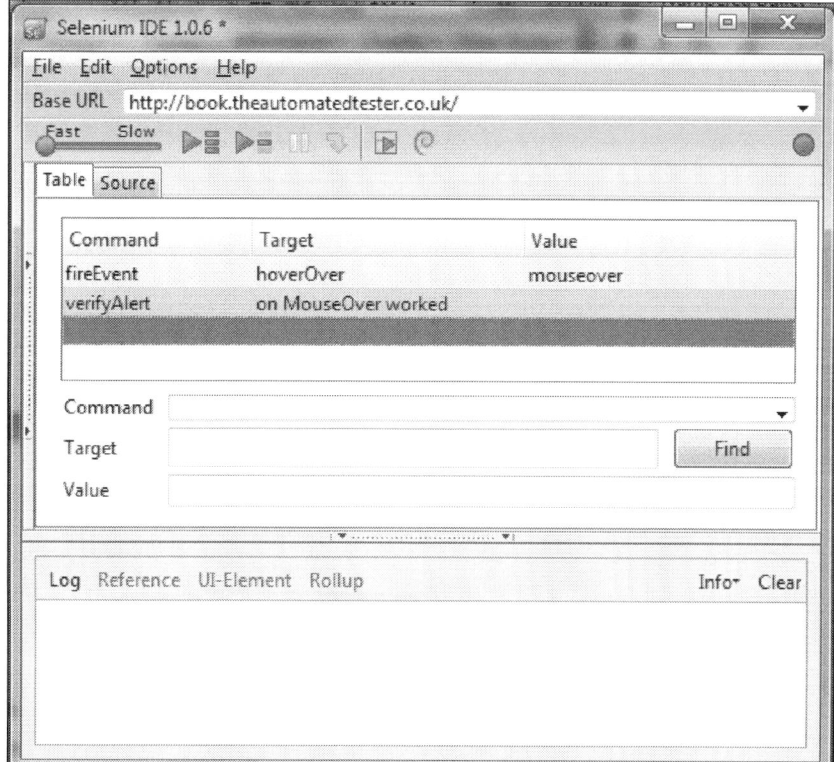

What just happened?

We have just seen how to fire an event by using the `fireEvent` command. This can be useful when Selenium cannot access the element or the command that you are using is just not firing the event.

Let's see how this can work with `onBlur`.

Time for action – firing an onBlur event in Selenium

Imagine that you have a form on a page that has some validation on the inputs. If you were to click away, it would validate that it matches what you would expect. Removing the focus will cause the `onBlur` to fire.

1. Open the Selenium IDE.
2. Navigate to `http://book.theautomatedtester.co.uk`.

3. Create a step to type in 'blurry'.
4. Create a step to `fireEvent` against blurry, the `onBlur` event alert for what you typed in the previous step.
5. Create a step to verify the alert.
6. Run your test. It should look similar to the next screenshot.

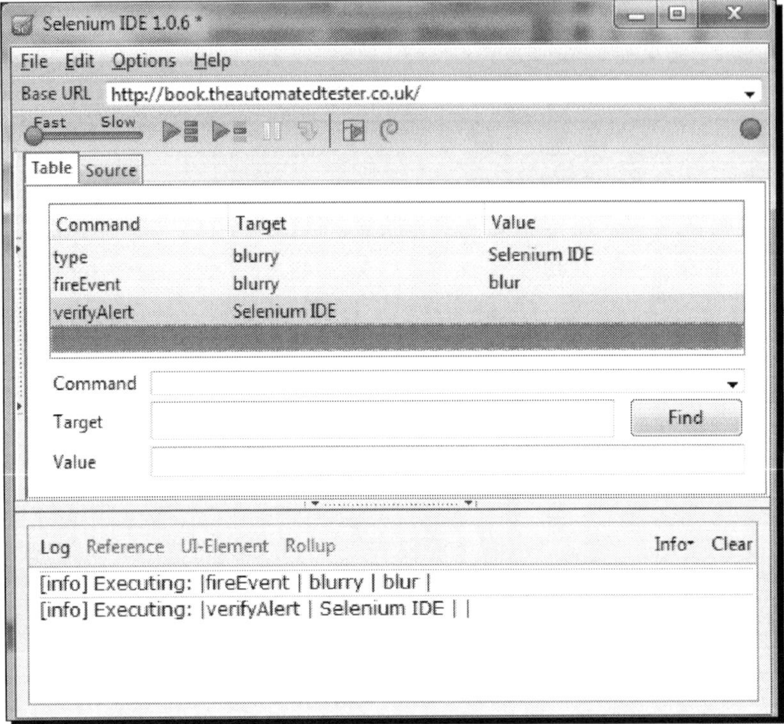

What just happened?

We just saw how we can fire an `onBlur` event during a test. This could be really useful for when you want to test client-side validation on a page. Form validation is one of the key parts to modern web applications either at the signup stage or on pages that need to be audited.

Summary

We learned a lot in this chapter about JavaScript and how we can use it within our tests. This can be really useful for those times where we can not use a standard Selenium command.

Specifically, we covered the following topics:

- **Using JavaScript**: In this section, we learned how to start using JavaScript in our tests. This was to make sure that we are always using the correct date when our tests run. This allows our Selenium tests to have a dynamic edge to them so that our tests do not have any hardcoded values, which make our tests brittle.
- **Using Selenium variables with our JavaScript**: In this section, we saw how to use variables that we created in Selenium IDE and then use them in our tests. We saw how we can read a number off a page using the `storeText` and then add a number. An example of this could be an auction site where you need to always pick a value that is larger than what is already selected.
- **Using browserbot**: There are times were we will need to access the page in our tests. This could be because we need to change something in the DOM, or we need to test some JavaScript API as part of a Selenium test. This is quite common, and as we saw, is not too difficult to achieve.
- **Using fireEvent in your tests**: In this section, we saw how to use the `fireEvent` command to make sure that our tests fire events that are attached to elements. This could be a `mouseOver` on an element that is difficult to access in your tests or if you wanted to test the blur or focus methods. These two methods and a couple of others cannot be tested directly with Selenium.

We also discussed how we can use the dynamic parts in our tests within assert or verify commands so that we can add more to the dynamism of our tests. This can help our tests to not be as brittle. When tests are not brittle, they can become invaluable.

Now that we've learned about using JavaScript in Selenium, we're ready to have a look at creating extensions and plugins for Selenium IDE—which is the topic of the next chapter.

5
User Extensions and Add-ons

In this chapter, we are going to look at how we can expand Selenium. This is for those times when Selenium's API is not verbose enough.

Selenium has the ability to allow developers to create functions, in the same three-column format, to all tests to reuse snippets of code instead of evaluating them with `getEval` *calls.*

User extensions and add-ons are all written in JavaScript. This is due to Selenium's core being written in JavaScript. Let's now have a look at user extensions.

In this chapter, we shall discuss:

- User extensions
- Add-ons

So let's get on with it...

Important preliminary points

If you are creating an extension that can be used by all, make sure that it is stored in a central place, like a version control system. This will prevent any potential issues in the future when others in your team start to use it.

User extensions

Imagine that you wanted to use a snippet of code that is used in a number of different tests. As we saw in the previous chapter, you could use:

```
type | locator | javascript{ .... }
```

However, if you had a bug in the JavaScript you would need to go through all the tests that reused this snippet of code.

This, as we know from software development, is not good practice and is normally corrected with a refactoring of the code. In Selenium, we can create our own function that can then be used throughout the tests.

User extensions are stored in a separate file that we will tell Selenium IDE or Selenium RC to use. Inside there the new function will be written in JavaScript.

Because Selenium's core is developed in JavaScript, creating an extension follows the standard rules for prototypal languages. To create an extension, we create a function in the following design pattern.

```
Selenium.prototype.doFunctionName = function(){
.
.
.
}
```

The "do" in front of the function name tells Selenium that this function can be called as a command for a step instead of an internal or private function.

Now that we understand this, let's see this in action.

Time for action – installing a user extension

Now that you have a need for a user extension, let's have a look at installing an extension into Selenium IDE. This will make sure that we can use these functions in future *Time for action* sections throughout this chapter.

1. Open your favorite text editor.
2. Create an empty method with the following text:

```
Selenium.prototype.doNothing = function(){
.
.
.
}
```

3. Start Selenium IDE.

4. Click on the **Options** menu and then click on **Options**.

5. Place the path of the `user-extension.js` file in the textbox labeled **Selenium IDE extensions**.

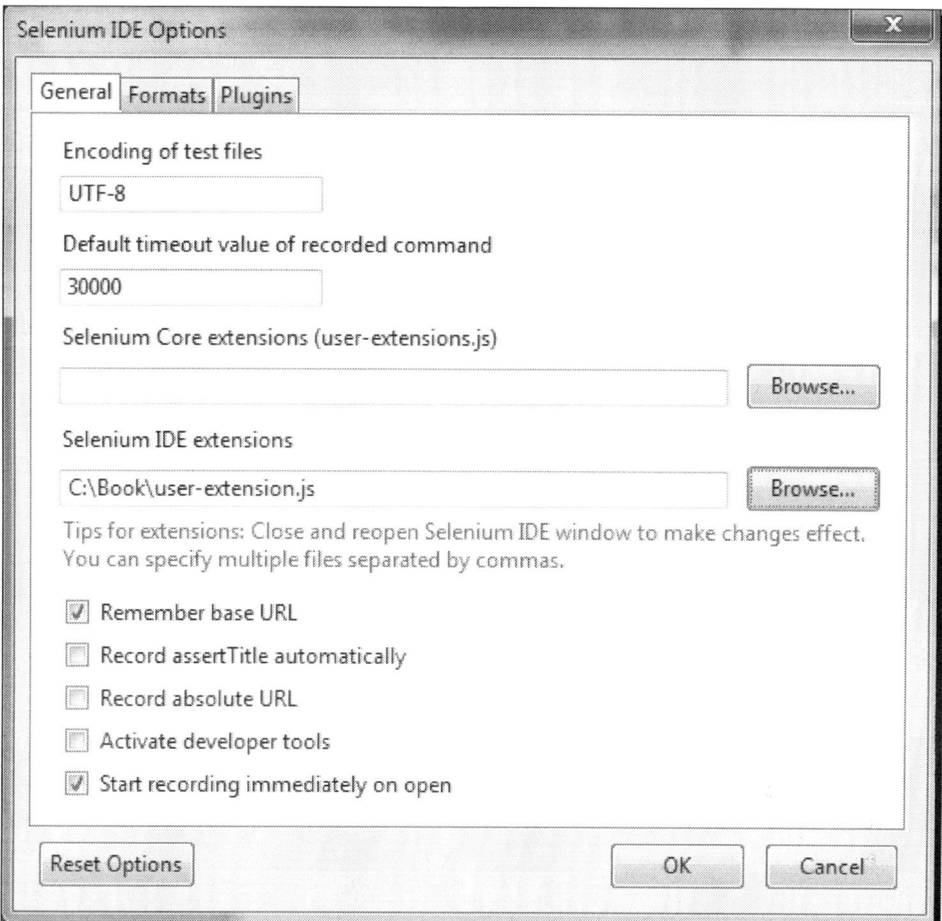

5. Click on **OK**.

6. Restart Selenium IDE.

7. Start typing in the **Command** textbox and your new command will be available, as seen in the next screenshot:

What just happened?

We have just seen how to create our first basic extension command and how to get this going in Selenium IDE. You will notice that you had to restart Selenium IDE for the changes to take effect. Selenium has a process that finds all the command functions available to it when it starts up, and does a few things to it to make sure that Selenium can use them without any issues.

Now that we understand how to create and install an extension command let's see what else we can do with it. In the next *Time for action*, we are going to have a look at creating a `randomizer` command that will store the result in a variable that we can use later in the test.

Time for action – using Selenium variables in extensions

Imagine that you are testing something that requires some form of random number entered into a textbox. You have a number of tests that require you to create a random number for the test so you can decide that you are going to create a user extension and then store the result in a variable.

To do this we will need to pass in arguments to our function that we saw earlier. The value in the target box will be passed in as the first argument and the value textbox will be the second argument. We will use this in a number of different examples throughout this chapter.

Let's now create this extension.

1. Open your favorite text editor and open the `user-extension.js` file you created earlier.
2. We are going to create a function called `storeRandom`. The function will look like the following:

   ```
   Selenium.prototype.doStoreRandom = function(variableName){
     random = Math.floor(Math.random()*10000000);
     storedVars[variableName] = random;
   }
   ```

3. Save the file.
4. Restart Selenium IDE.
5. Create a new step with `storeRandom` and the variable that will hold the value will be called `random`.

6. Create a step to echo the value in the random variable.

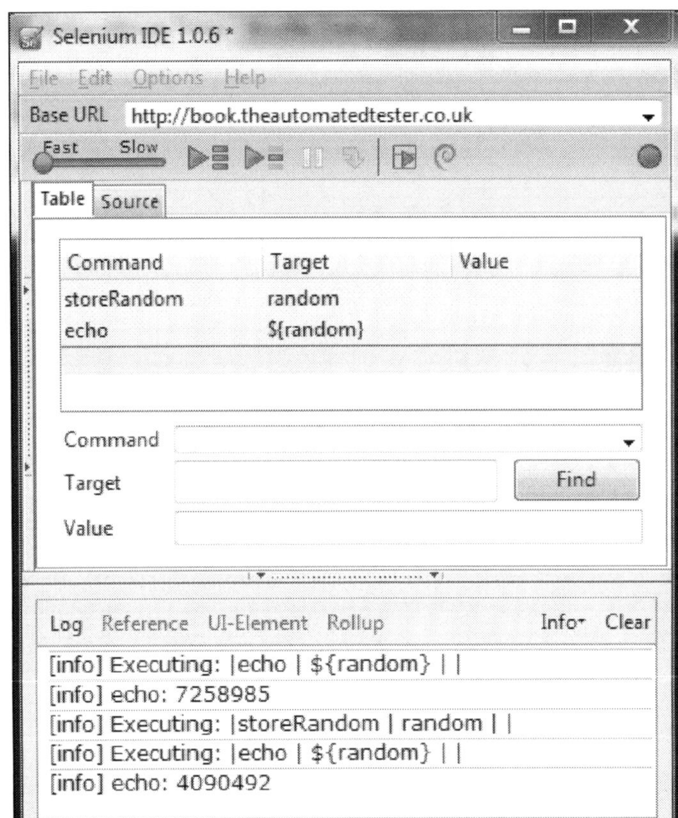

What just happened?

In the previous example, we saw how we can create an extension function that allows us to use variables that can be used throughout the rest of the test. It uses the `storedVars` dictionary that we saw in the previous chapter. As everything that comes from the Selenium IDE is interpreted as a string, we just needed to put the variable as the key in `storedVars`. It is then translated and will look like `storedVars['random']` so that we can use it later.

As with normal Selenium commands, if you run the command a number of times, it will overwrite the value that is stored within that variable, as we can see in the previous screenshot.

Now that we know how to create an extension command that computes something and then stores the results in a variable, let's have a look at using that information with a locator.

Time for action – using locators in extensions

Imagine that you need to calculate today's date and then type that into a textbox. To do that you can use the **type | locator | javascript{...}** format, but sometimes it's just neater to have a command that looks like **typeTodaysDate | locator**. We do this by creating an extension and then calling the relevant Selenium command in the same way that we are creating our functions. To tell it to type in a locator, use:

```
this.doType(locator,text);
```

The `this` in front of the command text is to make sure that it used the `doType` function inside of the Selenium object and not one that may be in scope from the user extensions.

Let's see this in action:

1. Use your favorite text editor to edit the user extensions that you were using in the previous examples.

2. Create a new function called `doTypeTodaysDate` with the following snippet:

```
Selenium.prototype.doTypeTodaysDate = function(locator){
  var dates = new Date();
  var day = dates.getDate();
  if (day < 10){
     day = '0' + day;
  }
  month = dates.getMonth() + 1;
  if (month < 10){
     month = '0' + month;
  }
  var year = dates.getFullYear();
  var prettyDay = day + '/' + month + '/' + year;
  this.doType(locator, prettyDay);

}
```

3. Save the file and restart Selenium IDE.

4. Create a step in a test to type this in a textbox.

5. Run your script. It should look similar to the next screenshot:

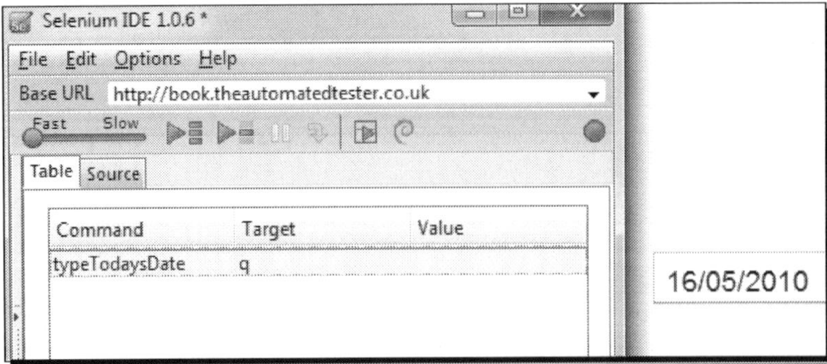

What just happened?

We have just seen that we can create extension commands that use locators. This means that we can create commands to simplify tests as in the previous example where we created our own `Type` command to always type today's date in the `dd/mm/yyyy` format. We also saw that we can call other commands from within our new command by calling its original function in Selenium. The original function has **do** in front of it.

Now that we have seen how we can use basic locators and variables, let's have a look at how we can access the page using browserbot from within an extension method.

Time for action – using browserbot from within an extension

Imagine that you need to interact with an element on the page and the only way to do that is to access it is through a JavaScript API. This is quite common when trying to automate testing against web-based editor components that are becoming commonplace. One that I have seen is the Telerik RADEditor.

To do this we will need to access the same `browserbot` object that we saw in the previous chapter, accessing it in the same way as we did in the previous chapter. This is because the `getEval` command runs the snippet within the Selenium object.

Let's see this in action now:

1. Open up your favorite text editor and open up the user extensions file that you created earlier.

2. Create a new function and call it `doCheckDate`, as seen in the following snippet:

```
Selenium.prototype.doCheckDate = function(){
var dates = new Date();
  var day = dates.getDate();
  if (day < 10){
     day = '0' + day;
  }
  month = dates.getMonth() + 1;
  if (month < 10){
     month = '0' + month;
  }
  var year = dates.getFullYear();
  var prettyDay = day + '/' + month + '/' + year;
  this.browserbot.getUserWindow().checkDate(prettyDay);
}
```

3. Save the file and restart Selenium IDE.

4. Create a new step using the new command.

5. Create a new step with `verifyText` that checks whether the location with "Answer" has the word `Correct`.

6. Run the script. It should look similar to the next screenshot:

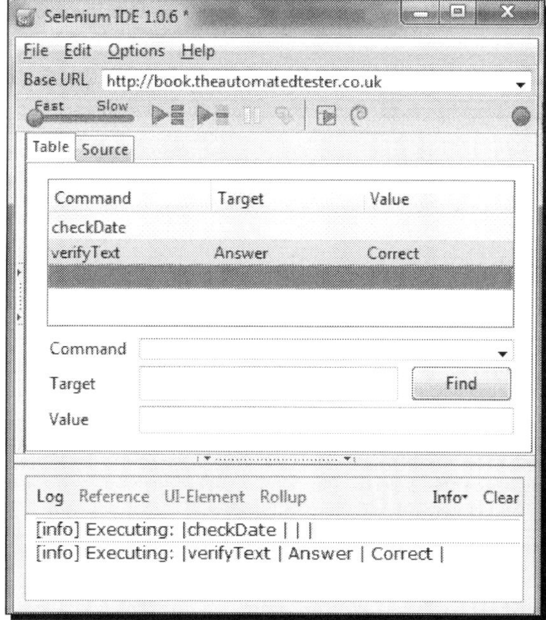

What just happened?

We have just seen how we can create a user extension to access the page using browserbot. This can then allow our tests to manipulate the DOM or access JavaScript APIs that may be available. Creating an extension command allows you to re-use the code in a number of different tests instead of using the `getEval` command.

This code re-use can be very beneficial especially if the tests require you to add or remove things from the DOM at the beginning of the test or at the end of the test.

There will be times where we may need to create a new command that either verifies or asserts something for the test. For this we can use the same technique Selenium's Core commands use to fail a test.

To do this we need to use the Selenium `CommandComplete` object in our extension method to keep track of the step when Selenium is updating the asserts passed or failed. This object is populated and then passed to the `commandComplete` function within the Selenium Object.

Let's now see this in action.

Time for action – creating new commands to verify or assert

Imagine that in the previous example you wanted to have the extension method verify the text on the screen instead of having a separate step to do the verification or assertion. This can make tests a lot more compact and possibly easier to read.

We can see this in the next example:

1. Open your favorite text editor and the user extensions file that you created earlier.
2. Create a new function called `doFireDateAndVerifyText` with the following snippet:

```
Selenium.prototype.doFireDateAndVerifyText =
function(locator,value){
var dates = new Date();
  var day = dates.getDate();
  if (day < 10){
     day = '0' + day;
  }
  month = dates.getMonth() + 1;
  if (month < 10){
     month = '0' + month;
  }
  var year = dates.getFullYear();
```

```
    var prettyDay = day + '/' + month + '/' + year;
    this.browserbot.getUserWindow().checkDate(prettyDay);

    var lastResult = new CommandResult();
    try{
     var realValue = this.getText(locator);

     if (realValue === value){
       lastResult.failed = false;
     } else {
       lastResult.failed = true;
     }
    } catch (e) {
      lastResult.failed = true;
      lastResult.message = e.message;
    }
    this.commandComplete(lastResult);
  }
```

3. Save the file and restart Selenium IDE.

4. Run the test. I have shown it being run against a page that will fail in order to show you that it can make the test fail.

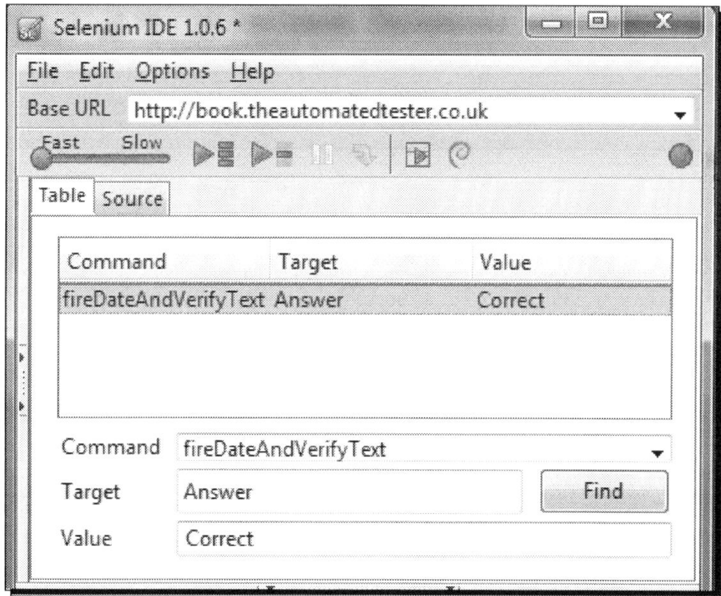

What just happened?

We have just seen how we can create new commands for our tests that can verify or assert that something is on the page. In the new command we started to use the `CommandResult` object to store the result of the test. When the step had completed, it called the `this.commandComplete` command so that we could record if the step was successful or not.

The `CommandComplete` object keeps track of whether the step was successful or not as well as any message that we may want to output to the screen to say why the step failed. This is the same procedure that Selenium Core code uses to show if a test has passed or failed.

If you wanted your new command to act as an *assert* and fail the test when it does not meet the criteria, add the following to the catch part of the extension:

```
this.testComplete();
```

Pop quiz

- How do you store variables to be used later in the test?
  - Use the `storedVars` dictionary
  - Create a new variable that has global scope
  - You cannot store variables using user extensions
- Can your user extension call other commands such as *type* or *click*?
- Can your user extension access the DOM programmatically?
- How can a new command fail a test if it was doing a *verify*?

Have a go hero – doing more with user extensions

Try to create a new command that will take a string from a variable that is saved in a step before and then reverse it. You will need to use the `storeText` command to get the string. Then create a function called `doReverse` that stores the result in a different variable to the one you used before. This second variable can then be echoed out or can be typed into a textbox or textarea.

Add-ons

Adam Goucher, one of the Selenium IDE maintainers, created a new API that allowed anyone to create new add-ons for Selenium IDE. These add-ons differ from the user extensions that we see all the time, in that they are Mozilla Firefox add-ons that Selenium can access. This is similar to the way that YSlow, a plugin from Yahoo! can access Firebug and give you all the information that is needed. We saw another add-on for Firebug called **Firefinder**.

Time for action – creating a basic add-on

In this section of the chapter, we are going to have a look at how we can make a basic add-on. The following steps can also be used to create a normal Firefox add-on.

Firstly, you will need to create a folder on your hard drive. I have called mine `Book`. Everything that follows will be done within that folder.

1. Open your favorite text editor.
2. Create a file called `install.rdf` and add the following snippet. This file tells Mozilla Firefox what is needed to install this add-on.

```
<?xml version="1.0" encoding="UTF-8"?>
<RDF xmlns="http://www.w3.org/1999/02/22-rdf-syntax-ns#"
     xmlns:em="http://www.mozilla.org/2004/em-rdf#">
  <Description about="urn:mozilla:install-manifest">
    <!-- needs to be in the format of an email address,
      but should be an actual email address -->
    <em:id>your email address</em:id>
    <!-- has to be lowercase -->
    <em:name>name of addon</em:name>
    <em:version>1.0</em:version>
    <em:creator>Your Name</em:creator>
    <em:description>
      A quick plugin for Selenium IDE
    </em:description>
    <em:type>2</em:type>
    <!--Preferences -->
    <em:optionsURL>
      chrome://book/content/view/options.xul
    </em:optionsURL>

    <!-- its a firefox plugin -->
    <em:targetApplication>
      <Description>
        <em:id>{ec8030f7-c20a-464f-9b0e-13a3a9e97384}</em:id>
        <em:minVersion>1.5</em:minVersion>
        <em:maxVersion>4.0.*</em:maxVersion>
      </Description>
    </em:targetApplication>

    <!-- this is an Se-IDE plugin,
      so we need to specify it as a requirement -->
    <em:requires>
```

```
        <Description>
          <em:id>{a6fd85ed-e919-4a43-a5af-8da18bda539f}</em:id>
          <em:minVersion>1.4</em:minVersion>
          <em:maxVersion>1.*</em:maxVersion>
        </Description>
      </em:requires>
    </Description>
  </RDF>
```

3. Create a new file called `chrome.manifest` in the root folder. Mine is `book`. This file lets the Mozilla Firefox add-on know where all the different bits of information are.

```
content book  chrome/content/

locale  book  en-US chrome/locale/en-US/

overlay chrome://selenium-ide/content/selenium-ide-common.xul
  chrome://book/content/view/optionsOverlay.xul
```

4. Now that we have created the call.
5. Create a folder called `content`.
6. Inside `content` create a folder called `view`.
7. Inside the `view` folder we will need to create a file called `optionsOverlay.xul` as we saw in the previous step. This will tell Selenium IDE that it needs to add the following items to the drop-down menu. The next snippet will add `Book Addon` options to the Selenium:

```
<?xml version="1.0"?>
<?xml-stylesheet href="chrome://global/skin/" type="text/css"?>

<overlay id="selenium_overlay"
xmlns=
  "http://www.mozilla.org/keymaster/gatekeeper/there.is.only.xul">

  <menupopup id="options-popup">
    <menuitem label="Book Addon options" accesskey="P"
      oncommand=
        "window.open('chrome://book/content/view/options.xul',
          'Book Options','chrome=yes,,centerscreen=yes');" />
  </menupopup>

</overlay>
```

8. Create a file called `options.xul` and place the following snippet in it:

```
<?xml version="1.0"?>
<?xml-stylesheet href="chrome://global/skin/" type="text/css"?>

<prefwindow id="book-prefs"
      title="'Book Options"
      width="520"
      height="200"
      xmlns=
  "http://www.mozilla.org/keymaster/gatekeeper/there.is.only.xul">

  <!-- Pref Pane -->
  <prefpane id="book-panel" label="'Book Options">

    <preferences>
      <preference id="pref_perform"
        name="extensions.selenium-ide.book.book-options"
        type="bool" />
    </preferences>
    <!—Window layout so we can see how it all works together -->
    <tabbox>
      <tabs>
        <tab label="General"/>
      </tabs>
      <tabpanels flex="1" >
        <tabpanel>
          <vbox flex="1">
            <hbox align="center">
<!—if you use & at the beginning and ; at the end it will allow
you to localize if you create a folder called locale in the root
and place in it different languages -->
              <label control="name" value="A Checkbox"/>
              <checkbox preference="checkbox_perf"
                id="checkbox" />
            </hbox>
            <spacer height="100" />
          </vbox>
        </tabpanel>
      </tabpanels>
    </tabbox>
  </prefpane>
</prefwindow>
```

9. In the `options.xul` file, you can add JavaScript so that when something is clicked, it can run a snippet of code. This means that you do not need to make something run automatically. To reference JavaScript you would add:

```
<!-- reference some javascript -->
<script type="application/x-javascript"
  src="chrome://selenium-ide/content/api.js"/>

<html:script type="application/javascript">
  var ide_api = new API();
  ide_api.addPluginProvidedFormatter("CheckBox",
    "Friendlier Checkbox name",
    "chrome://book/content/code/file-holding-info.js");
</html:script>
```

   This registers JavaScript to the item and then when it is clicked it will run that snippet of code.

10. Create a folder called `code` in `content`.

11. Create a file in `code` to hold your code snippet.

    To reference other JavaScript files, you will need to use the following syntax:

```
load('chrome://book/content/code/other-javascript.js');
```

    The snippet will need to have a name of what it will be recognized as. In the previous snippet, we called it `CheckBox`. Adding `this.name = 'Checkbox';` will do it. You can now add other functions that you may find useful.

12. When you have created everything you want, zip up the root folder. Mine is called `book`. Once this has been done, rename the file so that its file type is `.xpi`. The file type is normally the last three letters in the name that follows the last full stop.

Creating an add-on relies on understanding basic programming. You will need to understand how to develop using JavaScript because it is more than just creating the odd function we did in the previous section of the book.

What just happened?

We have just seen what it takes to create a new add-on that will attach to the Selenium IDE. This is a new bit of functionality that allows us to build onto IDE in a similar way to user extensions but can be a lot more powerful. This is because add-ons are not limited by the JavaScript sandbox.

Creating a new add-on requires programming knowledge that is slightly more intensive than creating extension methods that we saw previously.

Pop quiz

- What is a Selenium IDE add-on?

Summary

We learned a lot in this chapter about how we can extend Selenium when it does not have all the commands that we would want. This can be from needing a simple random number generator to a way to interact with a JavaScript API that is available on the page under test.

Specifically, we covered the following topics:

- **User extensions**: In this section of the chapter, we had a look at what is required to create a user extension. This gives us the ability to create new commands for our test steps. It gives us the ability to extend Selenium without having to rebuild Selenium from scratch.

  We had a look at how our extensions can use variables like we normally do within Selenium. This can be useful if you need to access an API and you only need to create the object once.

  We had a look at how we can call other commands from within our new command. This can be useful if we need to create a new a version of `Click` or `Type`.

  We briefly looked at how we can use the browserbot object within our extension and how this can benefit us if we need to create new commands to access JavaScript APIs on the page. And finally we had a look at how we can add verifications and assertions to our new commands so that if we are accessing an API, we can access it and verify in one command. This can make tests a lot more compact and easier to read.
- **Creating add-ons**: In this we saw how we can create a Mozilla Firefox add-on that can couple onto Selenium IDE. This will allow us to create tests that can use custom selectors or allow Selenium to work against items that it never has before, such as Flex. As this uses basic Firefox add-on design patterns, you can do a lot with it that can then be used to create new add-ons that do not need to be attached to Selenium IDE.

We also discussed that when saving user extensions we need to make sure that we restart the IDE after each save to make sure that it is always using the latest version.

Now that we've learned about user extensions, we're ready to have a look at Selenium RC—which is the topic of the next chapter. We should be extremely proficient with Selenium IDE by now, so moving on to Selenium RC allows us to create even more verbose tests.

6

First Steps with Selenium RC

In this chapter we are going to have a first look at Selenium Remote Control. Selenium Remote Control is one of the most popular flavors of Selenium as it allows developers to write tests using their favorite language to test on different Browsers.

In this chapter we shall cover topics such as:

- What is Selenium Remote Control
- Setting up Selenium Remote Control
- Running Selenium IDE tests with Selenium RC
- Selenium RC arguments

So let's get on with it...

Important preliminary points

To complete the examples of this chapter you will need to make sure that you have at least Java JRE installed. You can download it from `http://java.sun.com`. Selenium Remote Control has been written in Java to allow it to be cross platform, so we can test on Mac, Linux, and Windows.

What is Selenium Remote Control

In the previous chapters we have been using Selenium IDE, and by now you should be very proficient in using it. Selenium IDE only works with Firefox so we have only been checking a small subsection of the browsers that our users prefer. We, as web developers and testers, know that unfortunately our users do not just use one browser. Some may use Internet Explorer, others may use Mozilla Firefox. This is not to mention the growth of browsers such as Google Chrome and Opera.

Selenium Remote Control was initially developed by Patrick Lightbody as a way to test all of these different web browsers without having to install Selenium Core on the web server. It was developed to act as a proxy between the application under test and the test scripts. Selenium Core is bundled with Selenium Remote Control instead of being installed on the server.

This change to the way that Selenium tests are run allowed developers to interact with the proxy directly giving developers and testers a chance to use one of the most prominent programming languages to send commands to the browser.

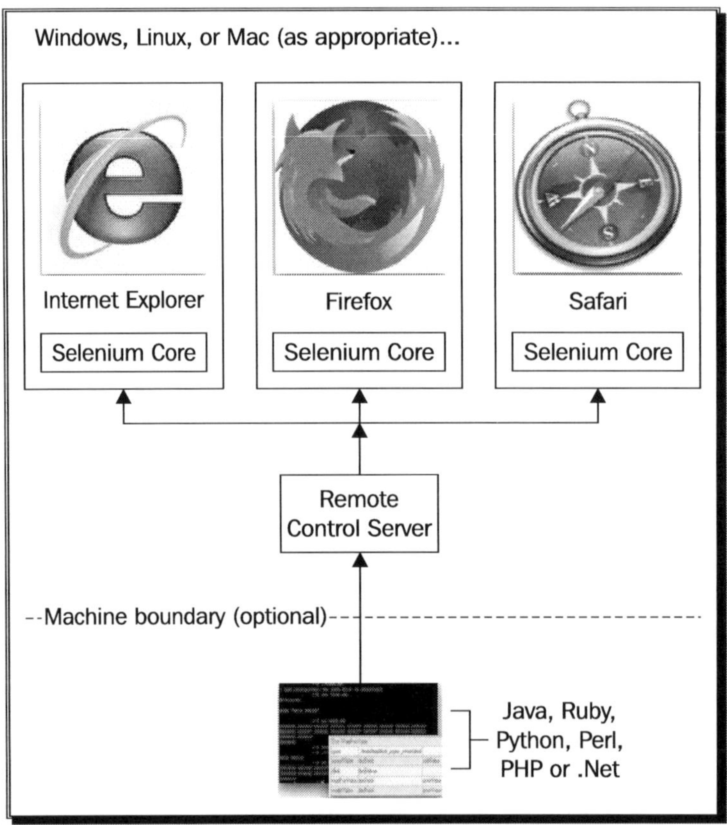

Java and C# have been the main languages used by developers to create Selenium Tests. This is due to most web applications being created in one of those languages. We have seen language bindings for dynamic languages being created and supported as more developers move their web applications to those languages. Ruby and Python are the most popular languages that people are moving to.

Using programming languages to write your tests instead of using the HTML-style tests with Selenium IDE allows you, as a developer or tester, to make your tests more robust and take advantage of all setups and tear down those that are common in most testing frameworks.

Now that we understand how Selenium Remote Control works, let us have a look at setting it up.

Setting up Selenium Remote Control

Selenium Remote Control is required on all machines that will be used to run tests. It is good practice to limit the number of Selenium Remote Control instances to one per CPU core. This is due to the fact that web applications are becoming more "chatty" since we use more AJAX in them. Limiting the Selenium instances to one per core makes sure that the browsers load cleanly and Selenium will run as quickly as possible.

Time for action – setting up Selenium Remote Control

1. Download Selenium Remote Control from `http://seleniumhq.org/download`.
2. Extract the ZIP file.
3. Start a Command Prompt or a console window and navigate to where the ZIP file was extracted.

4. Run the command `java -jar selenium-server-standalone.jar` and the output should appear similar to the following screenshot:

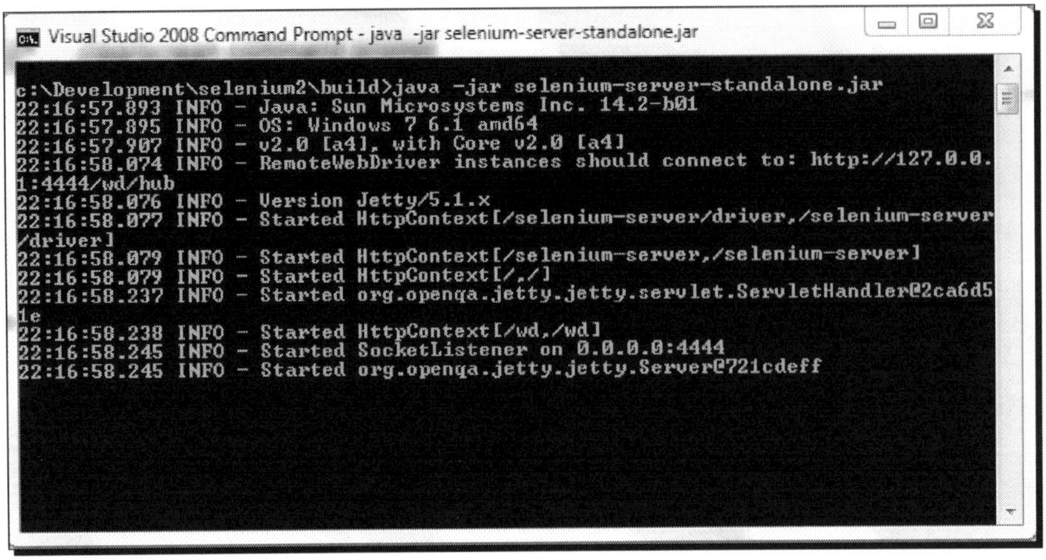

```
Visual Studio 2008 Command Prompt - java -jar selenium-server-standalone.jar

c:\Development\selenium2\build>java -jar selenium-server-standalone.jar
22:16:57.893 INFO - Java: Sun Microsystems Inc. 14.2-b01
22:16:57.895 INFO - OS: Windows 7 6.1 amd64
22:16:57.907 INFO - v2.0 [a4], with Core v2.0 [a4]
22:16:58.074 INFO - RemoteWebDriver instances should connect to: http://127.0.0.
1:4444/wd/hub
22:16:58.076 INFO - Version Jetty/5.1.x
22:16:58.077 INFO - Started HttpContext[/selenium-server/driver,/selenium-server
/driver]
22:16:58.079 INFO - Started HttpContext[/selenium-server,/selenium-server]
22:16:58.079 INFO - Started HttpContext[/,/]
22:16:58.237 INFO - Started org.openqa.jetty.jetty.servlet.ServletHandler@2ca6d5
1e
22:16:58.238 INFO - Started HttpContext[/wd,/wd]
22:16:58.245 INFO - Started SocketListener on 0.0.0.0:4444
22:16:58.245 INFO - Started org.openqa.jetty.jetty.Server@721cdeff
```

What just happened?

We have successfully set up Selenium Remote Control. This is the proxy that our tests will communicate with. It works by language bindings, sending commands through to Selenium Remote Control which it then passes through to the relevant browser. It does this by keeping track of browsers by having a unique ID attached to the browser, and each command needs to have that ID in the request.

Now that we have finished setting up Selenium Remote Control we can have a look at running our first set of tests in a number of different browsers.

Pop quiz – setting up Selenium Remote Control

- Where can you download Selenium Remote Control from?
- Once you have placed Selenium Remote Control somewhere accessible, how do you start Selenium Remote Control?

Running Selenium IDE tests with Selenium Remote Control

In the previous chapters we were using Selenium IDE to create all of our tests. This means that we have only been able to test our applications in Firefox. This means the testing coverage that you are offering is very limited. Users will use a number of different browsers to interact with your application. Browser and operating system combinations can mean that a developer or tester will have to run your tests more than nine times. This is to make sure that you cover all the popular browser and operating system combinations.

Now let's have a look at running the IDE tests that we created earlier with Selenium Remote Control.

Time for action – running Selenium IDE tests with Selenium Remote Control

Imagine that you have to run your Selenium IDE tests on a computer that doesn't have Selenium IDE installed or you do not want to use Firefox with any add-ons installed. To do this you will need to use Selenium Remote Control.

To run our tests in Selenium Remote Control we will have to use the `-htmlsuite` argument. This tells Selenium to open the Test Suite that we created. We then need to tell it where to find the Test Suite and then where to write the results to. Our command in Command Prompt or a console window will be similar to the following snippet:

```
Java -jar selenium-server-standalone.jar -htmlsuite *firefox http://book.
theautomatedtester.co.uk c:\path\to\testsuite.html c:\path\to\result.html
```

Let's try this with our test suite now.

1. Open a Command Prompt or console window.
2. Use the following command:

   ```
   Java -jar selenium-server-standalone.jar -htmlsuite *firefox
   http://book.theautomatedtester.co.uk "c:\book\chapter 6\testsuite.
   html" "c:\book\chapter 6\result.html"
   ```

I have placed my `testsuite` in `c:\book\chapter 6\`. Run this command and the output should look similar to the following screenshot:

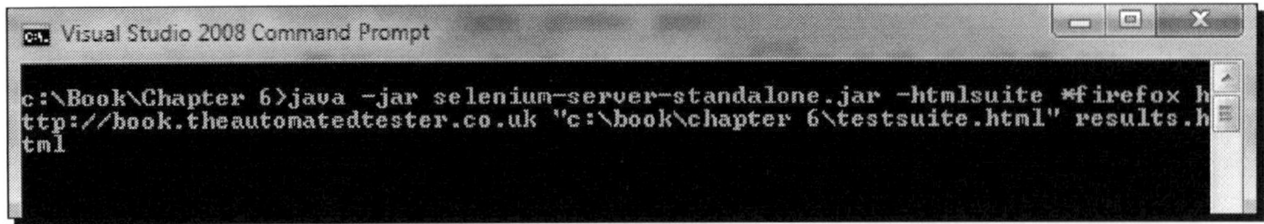

When the test starts running it will launch two browser windows. The first window will hold the Selenium Core Framework with the **Test Suite** on the left-hand side, the test steps in the center, and the results on the right-hand side. We can see what this looks like in the following screenshot:

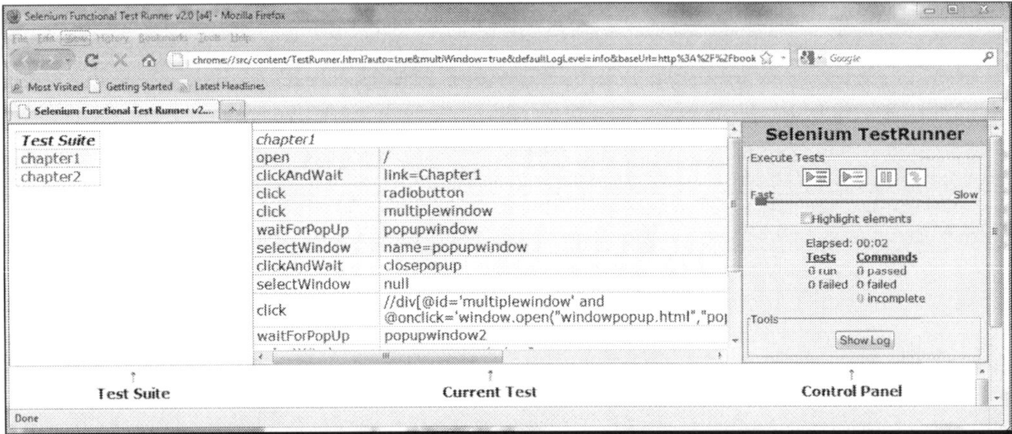

What just happened?

Using the `-htmlsuite` argument, we have managed to run our Selenium IDE tests through Selenium Remote Control. This time our tests used Firefox to run the Selenium IDE tests in Firefox. The command started Firefox and loaded the URL under test. It then loaded our test suite, and knows where to put the results when the tests are finished. When the tests have finished it will write the results to a file in a HTML format showing which tests have passed or failed and the command that it may have failed on. We can see what this looks like in the following screenshot:

Test suite results

result:	passed
totalTime:	4
numTestTotal:	2
numTestPasses:	2
numTestFailures:	0
numCommandPasses:	4
numCommandFailures:	0
numCommandErrors:	0
Selenium Version:	2.0
Selenium Revision:	a4

Test Suite
chapter1
chapter2

chapter1.html

chapter1		
open	/	
clickAndWait	link=Chapter1	
click	radiobutton	
click	secondajaxbutton	
verifyTextPresent	I have been added with a timeout	

chapter2.html

chapter2		
open	/	
clickAndWait	link=Chapter2	
verifyElementPresent	but1	
verifyElementPresent	//input[@value='Sibling Button']	
verifyElementPresent	//input[@name='verifybutton' and @value='chocolate']	

Running your Selenium IDE tests in Internet Explorer

Internet Explorer is one of the most popular browsers among users. Internet Explorer comes bundled with Microsoft operating systems, which is found on almost 90% of computers in the world. We, as developers and testers, should always be making sure that our code works on at least the latest variation of Internet Explorer but there are still people that use Internet Explorer 6, so be wary.

Time for action – running our tests in Internet Explorer

Now that we are aware that we need to make sure that our web applications work in Google Chrome, let us have a look at how we can make our Selenium IDE tests work on the same:

1. Open up a Command Prompt or console window.

2. Use the command `java -jar selenium-server.jar -htmlsuite *iexplore http://book.theautomatedtester.co.uk c:\path\to\testsuite.html c:\path\to\result.html` and press *Return*. When the browser has loaded it should look similar to the following screenshot:

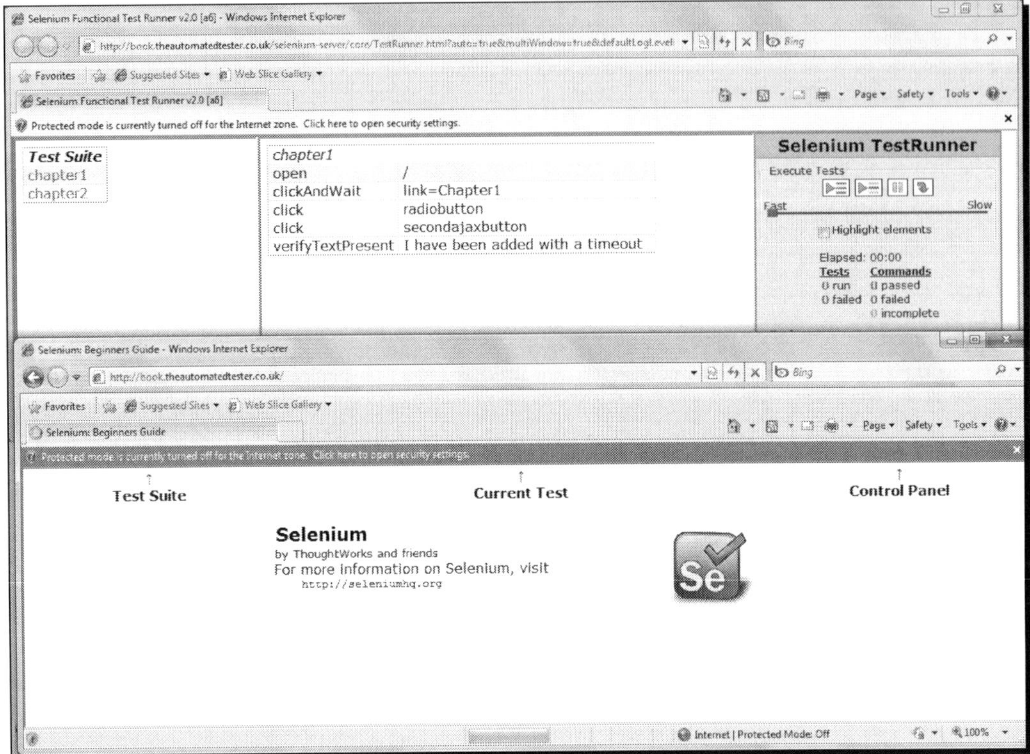

What just happened?

We have just seen how our tests run in Internet Explorer. This is the first time that we have run our tests against a browser that is not Mozilla Firefox. We have accomplished this without any changes to our tests. This one of the most powerful features of Selenium and why it is one of the favorite testing tools available. It allows us to extend test coverage to the two most used browsers on the planet.

Running your Selenium IDE tests in Google Chrome

Now that we have run our tests in both Internet Explorer and Mozilla Firefox, it is good to use a WebKit-based browser. The most popular browser of this type is Google Chrome. In this section we will have a look at running our Selenium IDE tests within Google Chrome. This will help us make sure that we have sufficient coverage of our application.

Time for action – running Selenium IDE tests within Google Chrome

Now that we have seen our tests work with two of the most popular browsers available, let's have a look at how it works with Google Chrome.

1. Open up a Command Prompt or console window.
2. Run the following command: `java -jar selenium-server.jar -htmlsuite *googlechrome http://book.theautomatedtester.co.uk c:\path\to\testsuite.html c:\path\to\result.html` and press *Return*. When the browser has loaded, it should look similar to the following screenshot:

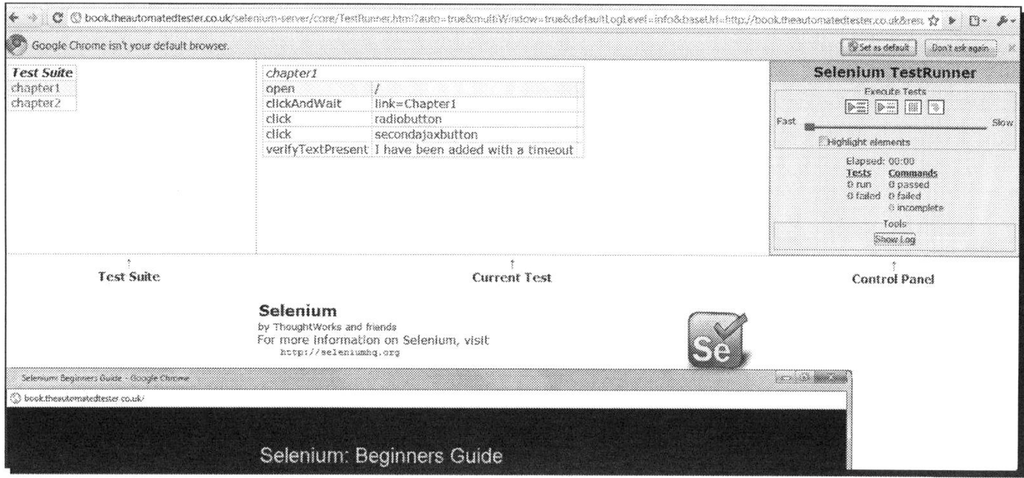

What just happened?

We have just seen how we can run our tests within Google Chrome. This means that we have, within this chapter, written one test suite and run it against three different browsers. This saves us, as developers or testers, a lot of effort in not having to create tests for each of the different browsers.

There are different types of browsers out there such as Opera and Konquerer to name two. We can see the browsers that are supported in the following list, and if your browser is not on the list, you can tell your test to use your `custom` browser with the path to your browser.

- `*firefox`
- `*mock`
- `*firefoxproxy`
- `*pifirefox`

- `*chrome`
- `*iexploreproxy`
- `*iexplore`
- `*firefox3`
- `*safariproxy`
- `*googlechrome`
- `*konqueror`
- `*firefox2`
- `*safari`
- `*piiexplore`
- `*firefoxchrome`
- `*opera`
- `*iehta`
- `*custom`

Running your Selenium IDE tests with the User Extensions

In the previous chapter we had a look at how we can create User Extensions. These are little commands that allow our tests to access different parts of the application.

Time for action – running Selenium IDE tests with User Extensions

Imagine that you have created a number of User Extensions and you would now like to use them in Selenium Remote Control tests that you have created by exporting your tests. The following steps will allow you to do this

1. Open a Command Prompt or console window.
2. Run the following command:

```
java -jar selenium-server-standalone.jar -userExtensions \\
path\to\extensions.js -htmlsuite *firefox http://book.
theautomatedtester.co.uk c:\path\to\testsuite.html c:\path\to\
results.html
```

What just happened?

We have just seen how we can use User Extensions with Selenium Remote Control. This means that our applications can not only be used on different browsers and platforms, but also use the new commands that we create in order to help us with our testing. This is one of the most popular arguments that people use.

Pop quiz

- Are you allowed to use relative paths to the Test Suite and results file?
- What is the argument needed to make your tests run within Firefox?
- What is the argument needed to make your tests run within Internet Explorer?
- What is the argument that allows our tests to use User Extensions?

Have a go hero

Now that you have seen your tests running in Mozilla Firefox, Internet Explorer, and Google Chrome, try running your tests in another browser. This can be from the list of supported browsers, or using the `*custom` attribute.

Selenium Remote Control arguments

The following is a list of the most common Selenium Remote Control arguments and how we can use them:

-port

Since Selenium Remote Control acts as a proxy between your tests and the application being tested, it has to use a port to listen for commands. There will be instances where you will not be able to use the standard 4444 port. When this happens, adding `-port <port number>` allows you to use a different port number without conflicts.

-userExtensions

We have already seen this in action. If you have created a user extension command in Selenium IDE, it can be used with Selenium Remote Control. By using `-userExtensions c:\path\to\file.js` we can access all the extra commands in our tests.

-firefoxProfileTemplate

If you require a special profile, or if you need to make sure that a specific Firefox Add-on is installed, use `-firefoxProfileTemplate /path/to/firefox/profile`. This command will take the profile that you want and then clone it to be used in your test.

Summary

In this chapter we had a look at Selenium Remote Control. This is the one tool in the Selenium suite of tools that truly allows us to write tests that are cross-platform and cross-browser. This will give us the confidence that our application works in all these different environments.

Specifically, we covered the following topics:

- **Selenium Remote Control**: We had a look at how Selenium Remote Control works. It is a proxy web server that sits between our tests which are running and the web application. This allows our tests to inject extra JavaScript to make the tests do the same as if we were using Selenium IDE.
- **Setting up Selenium Remote Control**: In this section of the chapter, we had a look at how we can set up Selenium Remote Control. We saw how Selenium Server and Selenium are just Java `.jar` files that can run from a Command Prompt.
- **Running Selenium IDE tests within Selenium Remote Control**: In this section of the chapter we had a look at how we can use all the test cases we created in previous chapters to test our web applications within Selenium Remote Control.
- **Selenium Remote Control arguments**: In this section we had a look at the rest of the Selenium Remote Control arguments that we may need in our tests.

Now that we've learned about the basics of Selenium Remote Control, we're ready to look at how we can use a programming language to make our tests a lot more robust. We can also harness items that are only available within programming languages—which is the topic of the next chapter.

7
Creating Selenium Remote Control Tests

In the previous chapter we had a look at setting up Selenium Remote Control on your computer. In this chapter we are going to have a look at converting your Selenium IDE tests into a programming language. This will allow us to create decent automated tests that are robust and extremely powerful. This is because we can use all the best parts of Selenium and the best parts of the programming language. Selenium Remote Control is the most popular variation of Selenium that is in use because of these facts.

In this chapter, we shall discuss the following topics:

- Converting Selenium IDE tests to run in a programming language and getting them running
- Writing Selenium Remote Control tests from scratch
- Applying best practices such as Page Object design pattern to create lasting tests
- Running tests against a continuous integration server

So let's get on with it...

Important preliminary points

In this chapter we will be writing our tests in Java. This is down to the popularity of the language by people using Selenium as well as its support on multiple platforms. To do this, we will need to have an IDE to write the tests in. I recommend using IDEA Intellij, as that is my favorite. You can download it from `http://www.jetbrains.com/idea/download/`, and I recommend it since it will give you all the tools that you need to build your tests successfully. If you already have Eclipse installed then this is just as good, but note the directions in this book are for IDEA Intellij, so they may not be exactly the same steps in Eclipse.

You will also need to download jUnit from `http://github.com/KentBeck/junit/downloads`. This will allow us to drive the tests and allow us to do asserts during the tests.

Converting Selenium IDE tests to a programming language

In the previous chapters we learnt how to create tests using Selenium IDE. This has been quite useful but we have not been able to take advantage of the best parts of testing frameworks such as `setUp` and `tearDown`.

Time for action – converting Selenium IDE tests to a language

We are going to be taking a Selenium IDE test and converting it into a Java test case. We will be using jUnit as the testing framework to drive our tests.

1. Open IDEA and create a new project.
2. Create a folder at the root of the project called `test`.
3. Click on **File | Project structure**.
4. Click on **Modules** on the left-hand side of the dialog that has loaded.
5. Click on the `test` folder that you created in the folder tree on the right-hand side of the dialog.
6. Click on the **Test Sources** button and the `test` folder should turn green. It will look like the following screenshot:

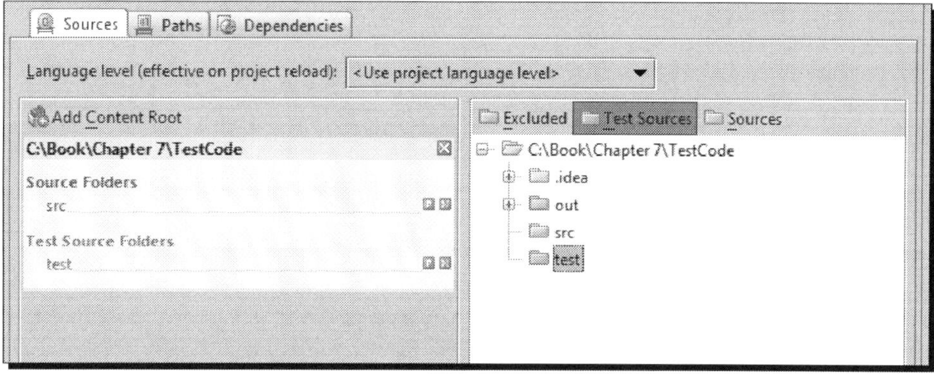

7. Open the Selenium IDE.

8. Open a Selenium IDE test you saved as HTML, or quickly create a new one.

9. Click on **File** then move the mouse pointer down to **Export Test Case As** and then click on **Java**.

In IDEA, it should look like this:

```
testcase1.java
package com.example.tests;

import com.thoughtworks.selenium.*;
import java.util.regex.Pattern;

public class testcase1 extends SeleneseTestCase {
    public void setUp() throws Exception {
        setUp("http://change-this-to-the-site-you-are-testing/", "*chrome");
    }
    public void testTestcase1() throws Exception {
        selenium.open("/");
        selenium.click("link=Chapter1");
        selenium.waitForPageToLoad("30000");
        selenium.select("selecttype", "label=Selenium RC");
        selenium.click("radiobutton");
        selenium.click("link=Home Page");
        selenium.waitForPageToLoad("30000");
        selenium.click("link=Chapter2");
        selenium.waitForPageToLoad("30000");
        verifyTrue(selenium.isElementPresent("//div[@id='divontheleft2']/input"));
    }
}
```

10. Change the text that says **change-this-to-the-site-you-are-testing** to **book.theautomatedtester.co.uk**. Our test is nearly ready. We are missing a few dependencies so let us now add these.

11. Click on **File | Project structure**.
12. Click on **Global libraries**.
13. Click on the **+** to add a **New Global library**.
14. Click on **Attach Classes** and add `selenium.jar` and `common.jar`. This should be in the same place as your `Selenium-Server.jar`. When added, it should look like this in the dialog:

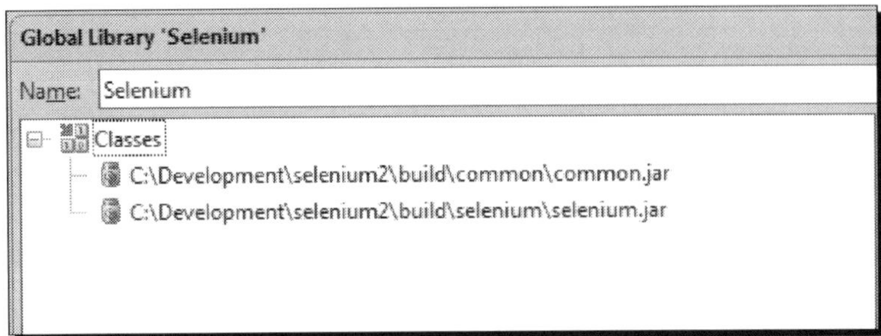

15. Do the same for jUnit now. You can create a new **Global** library for it or add it to the **Selenium Global Library**.
16. Click on the **Modules** link on the left-hand side again.
17. Click on the **Dependencies** tab.
18. Click on **Add** and click on **Global Libraries**. Add the Selenium and jUnit libraries.
19. Click on **Apply**. When this is done the text `selenium` should turn purple.
20. We are now ready to run Selenium Server. We do this by running `java-jar selenium-server.jar`.
21. Right-click on the Java file created by Selenium IDE and click on **Run "testcase1"** as in the screenshot:

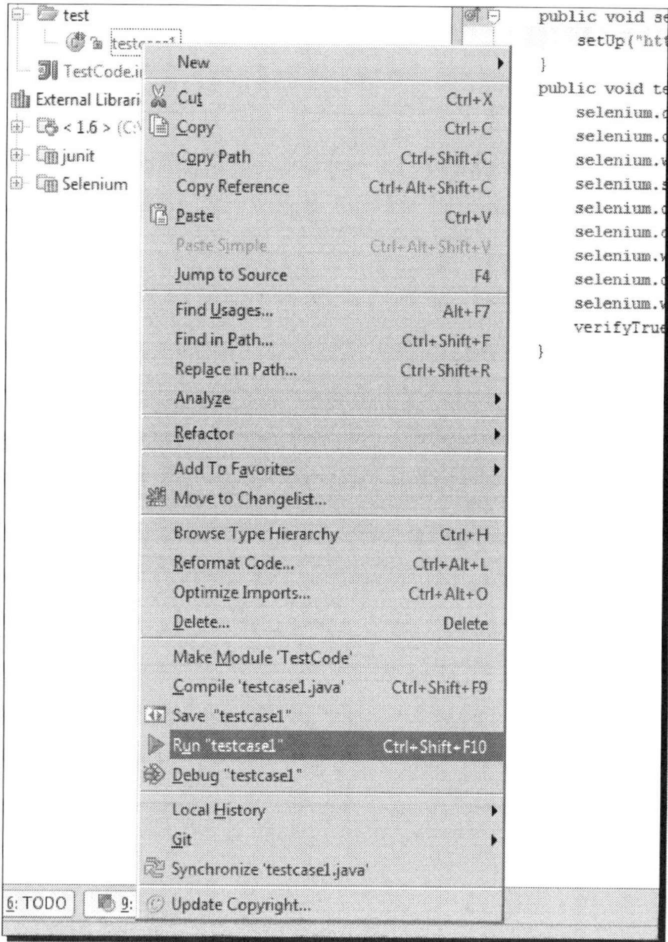

Your tests should start running now.

What just happened?

We have done a lot in this section. We had a look at how to set up IDEA for testing. This is a useful bit of information to know because it is useful to create tests for any form of Java project. The layout of the tests away from the source code allows us to separate concerns.

We then had a look at how we can export our Selenium IDE test to a programming language of choice. For this book I chose Java, but you could export your tests to Ruby, Java, C#, and Python. We saw what our test would look like within IDEA.

Copying our tests into IDEA will not allow our tests to run. This is just the text that is needed for the tests. We had a look at what dependencies are needed to get our tests running. We had a look at creating a global library to reference the Selenium JARs that we can reuse in any project that we need.

After getting all our dependencies filled we had a look at running our tests. Having got everything in place we were able to start running our tests. In this example we had our tests running in Mozilla Firefox but we could have had our tests running in any browser that we want. When our tests are running the browser will look slightly different to what we saw in the previous chapter. The Selenium Remote Control browser window will no longer show the test, it will show a command history of the commands that it has received. You can see this in the next screenshot:

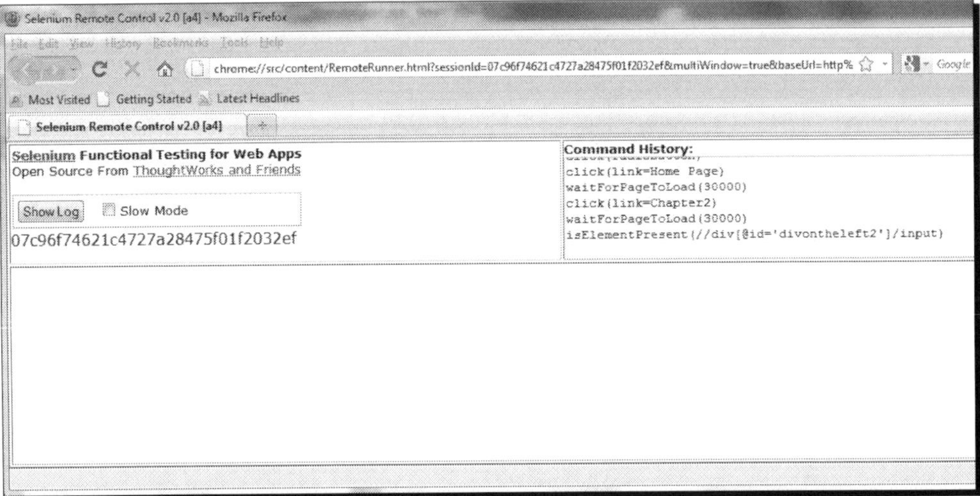

Pop quiz

- Do you need to create a folder for your tests?
- How does one export Selenium IDE tests into a programming language?
- Do you need to have Selenium JAR files as a dependency of your tests?
- How do you run your tests once the dependencies are correct?

Have a go hero – using different browsers

Once we had got our tests converted into Java, we ran them in Mozilla Firefox. Update the tests to use Google Chrome or Internet Explorer in your tests.

Writing Selenium tests from scratch

We have seen how we can create tests in Selenium IDE and then convert them to a programming language so that we can add things such as conditionals to our tests. Conditionals, logging, and disk access are all things that we can gain by using a programming language over Selenese. In this section we are going to have a look at how we can create tests from scratch so that we do not need to rely on Selenium IDE. If we, as developers or testers, need to update our tests within Selenium IDE and then export them to a programming language, we are going to be adding an unnecessary maintenance cost. There is the other negative aspect, Selenium IDE exports each test into separate files. This can be quite annoying when you are testing a behavior but with code paths.

By the end of this section you will understand how to create a `selenium` object and have it start a browser. For the rest of the book when I mention a Selenium instance it will be a Selenium Object and then starting the browser. Let's have a look at how we can create a Selenium Instance.

Time for action – creating a Selenium instance with JUnit 3

When you need to create a new Selenium instance you will need to do a few things depending on what version of JUnit you are using. In this *Time for action* we are going to be creating our tests using JUnit 3. Let us have a look at how we can create our tests:

1. Create a new java class in IDEA.
2. Add the Selenium Import to your java class:

   ```
   import com.thoughtworks.selenium.*;
   ```

3. For JUnit 3, we need to extend our java class with the `TestCase` class.

   ```
   public class SeleniumBeginnersJUnit3 extends TestCase {
     Selenium selenium;
   }
   ```

4. We now need to set up a new Selenium instance. We will do this in the `setUp` method that is run before the tests. In this we will initialize the `selenium` object that we previously created. This object takes four parameters in the constructor. They are:
   - Machine name hosting the Selenium Remote Control server.
   - Port that Selenium Remote Control server is running.
   - Browser string. For example `*chrome`.
   - Site under test.

The following code shows the initialization:

```
selenium = DefaultSelenium("localhost",4444,"*chrome",
  http://book.theautomatedtester.co.uk);
```

5. Let's start the browser up programmatically. We do this by calling the `start()` method.

   ```
   selenium.start();
   ```

   Your `setUp()` method should look like the following snippet:

   ```
   public void setUp(){
           selenium = new DefaultSelenium("localhost",4444,"*chrome",
             "http://book.theautomatedtester.co.uk");
           selenium.start();
   }
   ```

6. Now we need to create a test method. We do this by creating a new method that has `test` as a prefix. For example: `testShouldDoSomething(){…}`.

7. We can add `selenium` commands in our test so that it can drive the browser. For example:

   ```
   public void testShouldOpenChapter2LinkAndVerifyAButton(){
           selenium.open("/");
           selenium.click("link=Chapter2");
           selenium.waitForPageToLoad("30000");
           Assert.assertTrue(selenium.isElementPresent("but1"));
   }
   ```

8. Right-click on the test method and click on **Run Test**. You should see your test driving the browser.

What just happened?

We have just created a Selenium test and run it using JUnit 3. We saw how we can extend `TestCase` with our class and then set up a new `selenium` instance. We also saw how we can then stop the browser by calling the `stop()` method. We also saw that if you are creating a test you need to put 'test' as the prefix of the method. For example:

```
public void testShouldOpenChapter2LinkAndVerifyAButton(){
```

Time for action – creating a Selenium instance with SeleneseTestCase setUp()

In the previous section we saw how we can explicitly set all the properties that are needed to start a browser. We will now use the setup override in `SeleneseTestCase` to use certain values. The steps are as follows:

1. Create a new java class in IDEA.
2. Add the Selenium Import to your java class.

   ```
   import com.thoughtworks.selenium.*;
   ```

3. For JUnit 3, we need to extend our java class with the `TestCase` class. Selenium has its own version of the `TestClass` called `SeleneseTestCase`.

   ```
   public class SeleniumBeginnersJUnit3 extends SeleneseTestCase {

   }
   ```

4. We now need to set up a new Selenium instance. We will do this in the `setUp` method that is run before the tests. In this we will initialize the `selenium` object that we created previously. This method takes two parameters. These are:
   - Browser string. For example `*chrome`.
   - Site under test.

   The following code shows the initialization:

   ```
   setUp("*chrome",http://book.theautomatedtester.co.uk);
   ```

5. Now we need to create a test method. We do this by creating a new method that has `test` as a prefix. For example: `testShouldDoSomething(){…}`.
6. We can add `selenium` commands in our test so that it can drive the browser. For example:

   ```
   public void testShouldOpenChapter2LinkAndVerifyAButton(){
           selenium.open("/");
           selenium.click("link=Chapter2");
           selenium.waitForPageToLoad("30000");
           Assert.assertTrue(selenium.isElementPresent("but1"));
   }
   ```

7. Right-click on the test method and click on **Run Test**. You should see your test driving the browser.

What just happened?

We have just allowed Selenium to use a number of defaults. The main default was that it expects Selenium Remote Control to be running on the same machine as the tests. You can also use the other override which assumes that you are using Mozilla Firefox as the browser. This override only takes the site under test.

Now that we have created tests in JUnit 3, let's have a look at how we can create tests in the new JUnit 4 style.

Time for action – creating a Selenium instance with JUnit 4

Starting a browser is the most important part of Selenium for obvious reasons so let us have a look at doing that. In this *Time for action* we will be creating a new instance using JUnit 4.

1. Create a new java class in IDEA.
2. Import the Selenium and JUnit. You can the use the following code:
   ```
   import com.thoughtworks.selenium.*;
   import org.junit.*;
   ```
3. We now need to start a browser. You will need to declare a Selenium variable. Do this outside of any method.
4. Create a new method that will be run before any of the tests. Inside that we will start our `selenium` instance. Your code will look similar to the following:
   ```
   @Before
   public void setUp(){
           selenium = new DefaultSelenium("localhost",4444,"*chrome",
             "http://book.theautomatedtester.co.uk");
           selenium.start();
   }
   ```
   The `.start()` call will make Selenium start the browser up
5. Now that we can start up the browser, we will also need to kill it when our test has finished. We do this by creating a `@After` method with `selenium.stop()` in it. The method will look similar to the following:
   ```
   @After
   public void tearDown(){
           selenium.stop();
   }
   ```

Your test file should look like this now

```
import com.thoughtworks.selenium.*;
import org.junit.*;

public class Selenium2 {

    Selenium selenium;

    @Before
    public void setUp(){
        selenium = new DefaultSelenium("localhost",4444,"*chrome",
          "http://book.theautomatedtester.co.uk");
        selenium.start();
    }

    @Test
    public void shouldOpenChapter2LinkAndVerifyAButton(){

    }

    @After
    public void tearDown(){
        selenium.stop();
    }
}
```

6. Run the test by right-clicking and clicking on **Run Test** in the context menu.

What just happened?

When you have run the last step, you will see the browser start up and then disappear. The `DefaultSelenium` object takes four parameters in its constructor:

- Machine name where the Selenium Remote Control live exists.
- The port that Selenium Remote Control is running on.
- The browser that you want to launch. This is the same list that we saw in the previous chapter.
- The last parameter is the URL under test.

We then started the browser by calling the `start()` function. This will launch the browser and when we are finished we will need to then call the `stop()` function. This will kill off the browser process. Killing the process will allow us to then start it up again with the Selenium Remote Control and get a clean browser environment for the next test.

If you want to use TestNG to run your tests it will not take too much effort to change your JUnit tests to TestNG tests. In the *Time for action* section next, we will create a TestNG test.

Time for action – creating a Selenium instance with TestNG

TestNG is another extremely popular testing framework for Java. It can be more extensible than JUnit. We will be using TestNG in later chapters for parallelizing the running of our tests on Selenium Grid, but for now let us have a look at creating a test.

1. Create a new class file for testing against `http://book.theautomatedtester.co.uk/`.
2. Create a new `setUp` method. Use the annotation `@BeforeMethod`. This will need to have the code to start a Selenium instance.
3. Create a new `tearDown` method. Use the annotation `@AfterMethod`. This will need to have the code to close a Selenium Instance.
4. Create a new test. This uses the same annotation as JUnit 4.
5. When you have completed that your test file should look like this:

```
package uk.co.theautomatedtester.book;

import com.thoughtworks.selenium.DefaultSelenium;
import com.thoughtworks.selenium.Selenium;
import org.testng.annotations.*;

public class Chapter10 {

    Selenium sel;

    @BeforeMethod(alwaysRun=true)
    public void setUp(){
        sel = new DefaultSelenium("localhost",4444,browser,
          "http://book.theautomatedtester.co.uk");
        sel.start();
    }

    @Test
    public void testShouldOpenTheRootOfSite(){
        sel.open("/");
    }

    @AfterMethod
    public void tearDown(){
        sel.stop();
    }
}
```

6. Run the test. You do this the same way that you do in JUnit and IDEA by right-clicking on the test and then clicking on **Run Test** in the context menu that loads.

What just happened?

We have successfully created a test using the TestNG annotation within our Java code. There is very little difference in the way that JUnit and TestNG work except that it can give a little more extensibility, especially when we want to run our tests in parallel in Selenium Grid.

Now that we know how to get a Selenium instance going, let's have a look at creating a test.

Time for action – creating a test from scratch

We have created all the scaffolding needed for our tests so now we need to create the tests. In our class that we created in the previous Time for action we will need to create a new method and place the `@Test` as the attribute of the method. Let us create an example that loads the site root and then moves to the `chapter2` page and verifies a button on the page. Most of the Selenium IDE commands port across without any changes. The Asserts and Verifies use the testing frameworks assert methods.

1. Create a new method. I have called mine `shouldOpenChapter2LinkAndVerifyAButton`. Add the `@Test` attribute to that method.
2. Use the `open()` function and open the `root (/)` of the site.
3. Click on the link for `Chapter2`.
4. You will need to call the `waitForPageToLoad()` method to wait for it to load. This method takes one parameter and that is how long Selenium should wait for it to load before throwing an error.
5. Finally `Assert` that the button `but1` is on the screen. This will need to use JUnit's `Assert` class. You will need to call Selenium's `isElementPresent` call and wrap that with `assertTrue`.

   When your test is complete it should appear as follows:

```
@Test
public void shouldOpenChapter2LinkAndVerifyAButton(){
    selenium.open("/");
    selenium.click("link=Chapter2");
    selenium.waitForPageToLoad("30000");
    Assert.assertTrue(selenium.isElementPresent("but1"));
}
```

What just happened?

We have just managed to create our first test without any help from Selenium IDE. You have been able create a test that can be modified to add new steps with little fuss.

Pop quiz

- How many parameters does the Selenium object take when using DefaultSelenium?
- What class do we need to extend when writing JUnit 3 style tests?
- If we are running Selenium Server, can we use a different `setUp()` method?
- How do you start the browser?
- How do you stop the browser?
- How do I do asserts and verifies when writing tests in a programming language?

Have a go hero

Try taking all of your Selenium IDE tests and manually converting them to a test in Java. If you don't want to start a browser at the beginning of each test you can use the `@BeforeClass` and kill it in the `@AfterClass`.

Selenium Remote Control best practises

In this section of the chapter we are going to have a look at how we can apply some best practices to tests. You will learn how to make maintainable test suites that will allow you to update tests in seconds. We will have a look at creating your own DSL so that people can see intent. We will create tests using the Page Object Pattern.

Let us start trying to put these best practices to work.

Time for action – setting up the test

Imagine that you have a number of tests that work on a site that requires you to log in and move to a certain page. Or imagine that you need to have a test that requires you to be on a certain page. In these two situations the quickest way is to find out which page you are on and then move to the correct one, if need be, otherwise start testing. This is to make sure that we follow one of the major tenets of test automation in that you always start from a known place. Let us see this in an example:

1. Create a new java class in IDEA.
2. Import the relevant Selenium Packages.

3. Create the `setUp()` and `tearDown()` method. I prefer the JUnit 4 style of tests and so will use code samples with the annotations.

4. We need to check that the test is on the correct page. For this we will use the `selenium.getTitle` to see that page title, and then if incorrect move to the `chapter2` link. We do this because navigating to page is slower than checking the page's title or any other calls to the page already loaded.

5. We need to then validate that it is correct and then work accordingly. The following code snippet is an example of how we can do this:

```
if (!"Page 2".equals(selenium.getTitle())){
            selenium.open("/chapter2");
            selenium.waitForPageToLoad("30000");
        }
```

6. Create the rest of the test to check that items are on the page.

What just happened?

We have just seen how we can check that something is what the test is expecting. If it is, the test will carry on as we expect. If it isn't what we expect we can move our test to the correct page and then carry on the test. We will see that if you login in the `@Before` you may not start your tests.

Now let's have a look at how we can make more tests maintainable by splitting areas out into other methods.

Time for action – moving Selenium steps into Private methods to make tests maintainable

Imagine that you just need to test one page on your site and you have quite a few tests for this page. A lot of the tests will be using the same code over and over. This can be quite annoying to maintain if something changes on the page and you have to go through all the tests to fix this one issue. The way that we will fix this is to refactor the tests so they are simpler and by proxy easier to read.

Let us create a number of tests as follows:

```
@Test
public void shouldCheckButtonOnChapter2Page(){
         selenium.open("/");
        selenium.click("link=Chapter2");
        selenium.waitForPageToLoad("30000");
        Assert.assertTrue(selenium.isElementPresent("but1"));
```

```
    }
    @Test
    public void shouldCheckAnotherButtonOnChapter2Page(){
        selenium.open("/");
        selenium.click("link=Chapter2");
        selenium.waitForPageToLoad("30000");
        Assert.assertTrue(selenium.isElementPresent("verifybutton"));
    }
```

Using the given examples let's break these down.

1. Both examples always open the root of the site. Let's move that into its own private method. To do this in IDEA you highlight the lines you want to refactor and then right-click. Use the context menu and then **Extract Method**.

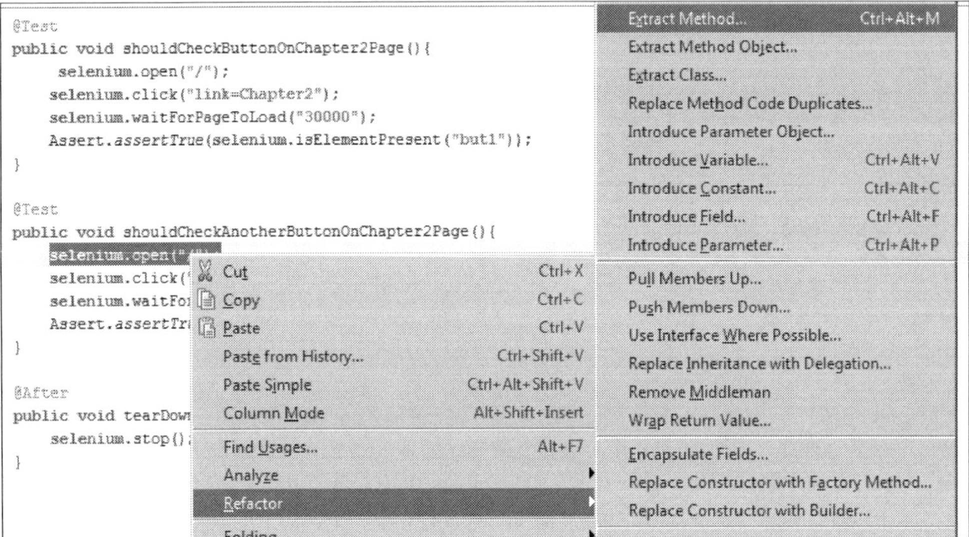

2. Then you will see a dialog asking you to give the method a name. Give it something meaningful for the test. I have called it **loadHomePage** as you can see in the next screenshot:

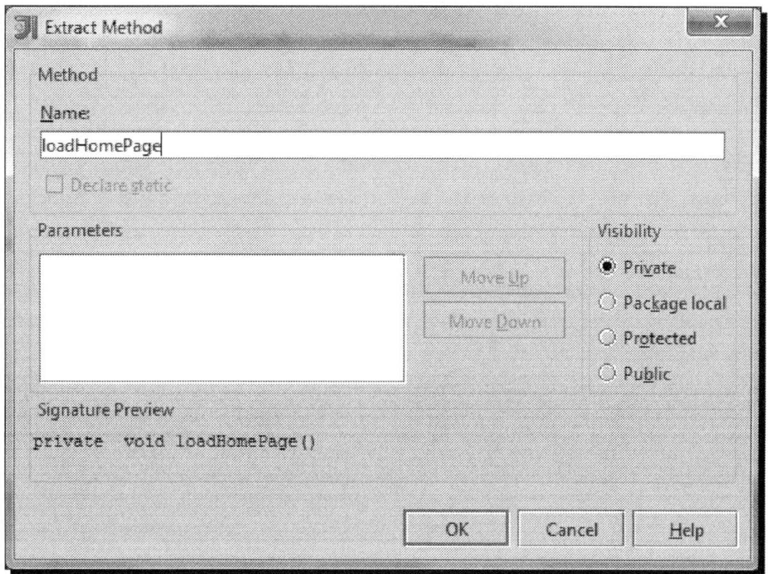

3. Now do the same for the other parts of the test so that it looks a lot more succinct.

4. Your test class should look something like this:

```
@Test
public void shouldCheckButtonOnChapter2Page(){
    loadHomePage();
    clickAndLoadChapter2();
Assert.assertTrue(selenium.isElementPresent("but1"));
}

@Test
public void shouldCheckAnotherButtonOnChapter2Page(){
    loadHomePage();
    clickAndLoadChapter2();
    Assert.assertTrue(selenium.isElementPresent("verifybutt
on"));
}

private void loadHomePage() {
    selenium.open("/");
}

private void clickAndLoadChapter2() {
    selenium.click("link=Chapter2");
    selenium.waitForPageToLoad("30000");
}
```

What just happened?

We have just started making our tests a lot more maintainable. We saw how we can break this down into more succinct and readable tests that show intent rather than showing a test as a clump of Selenium calls. This also makes the tests a lot more manageable because if I were to change the link on the root from "Chapter2" to "Chapter 2" I would need to only fix it in one place rather than n places where n is the number of times that sequence is in the test class.

Now let's have a look at how we can use the Page Object Pattern for creating a DSL over the site.

Time for action – using the Page Object Pattern to design tests

Imagine that you have a site that has a number of different pages that you need to test. This is quite common for a number of sites. We can create an object that represents the page and then pass the Selenium object in the programming language. So let us now create our first Page Object against the Home page.

1. Create a new Java class in IDEA called `HomePage`.
2. Import the relevant packages for the tests to run.
3. We will now need a constructor to handle Selenium. You may want to make it go to the home page when it is instantiated too. An example of this can be as follows:

   HomePage.java

   ```
   import com.thoughtworks.selenium.Selenium;

   public class HomePage{
     Selenium selenium;
       public HomePage(Selenium selenium){
       this.selenium = selenium;
     }
     public Chapter2 clickChapter2(){
       clickChapter("2");
       selenium.waitForPageToLoad("30000");
           return new Chapter2(selenium);
     }

       private void clickChapter(String number){
           selenium.click("link=Chapter"+number);
       }
   }
   ```

Chapter2.java

```
import com.thoughtworks.selenium.Selenium;
import junit.framework.Assert;

public class Chapter2 {
    Selenium selenium;
    public Chapter2(Selenium selenium){
        this.selenium = selenium;
        if (!"Chapter 2".equalsIgnoreCase(
          this.selenium.getTitle())
        ){
            selenium.open("/chapter2");
        }
    }
    public void assertButton(String button){
        Assert.assertTrue(selenium.isElementPresent(button));
    }
}
```

BestPractises3.java

```
import com.thoughtworks.selenium.*;
import org.junit.*;

public class BestPractises3 {
    Selenium selenium;

    @Before
    public void setUp(){
        selenium = new DefaultSelenium("localhost",4444,"*chrome",
          "http://book.theautomatedtester.co.uk/");
        selenium.start();
    }

    @After
    public void tearDown(){
        selenium.stop();
    }

    @Test
    public void ShouldLoadTheHomePageAndThenCheckButtonOnChapter2()
   {
        HomePage hp = new HomePage(selenium);
        Chapter2 ch2 = hp.clickChapter2();
```

```
            ch2.assertButton("but1");
        }
    }
```

If you create these three files, you will see the test pass. The test is a lot more succinct and easier to maintain.

What just happened?

In this section we had a look at creating tests using the Page Object design pattern. This allows us to create objects in a programming language and then pass the `selenium` object to it to drive the browser. This creates a really nice DSL that allows all parties in the development cycle to understand. We create a Java object for each of the pages that we want to work against on the site. We then just instantiate the class to work against that page.

When we are moving between pages you click on a link, and the method controlling the page transition will return an object representing a new page.

The objects will not hold the asserts, this should always be done within the tests.

Pop quiz

- What is the Page Object design pattern?

Have a go hero

Now that you can confidently create manageable tests, why not go through all the tests that you created when exporting them from Selenium IDE and try to make them maintainable. You can refactor all the bits of code that look the same.

Setting our tests up in a Continuous Integration server

The final section of this chapter is on how we can get our tests running on a Continuous Integration server. This is the most common way to run tests as it will get done every time that you do a commit to your version control system. We will be looking at how we can set up an Ant Task as that is understood by most Continuous Integration applications.

Let's see how we can set up our Ant Task.

Time for action – creating an Ant file

To get our Continuous Integration server to use Ant we will need to create a file and populate it. It will contain different aspects so we will break it down starting with the shell and then adding things as we need them.

1. Create a file called `tests.xml` and in it put the XML blob given next. This will give us a project to work in. Set the values for properties for items that you are working with.

```
<?xml version="1.0" encoding="UTF-8"?>
<project name="Run Test" default="run_test" basedir=".">

    <property name="test.dir" value="src\test" />
      <!—This is where our tests live -->

    <property name="testLibDir" value="lib" />
      <!—This is where Selenium RC lives -->
</project>
```

2. We now need to add a snippet to start and stop the Selenium Remote Control server. To do that we need to add the following snippet below the `property` nodes.

```
<target name="start-server">
  <java jar="lib/selenium-server.jar"
    fork="true" spawn="true">
  </java>
</target>

<target name="stop-server">
  <get taskname="selenium-shutdown"
    src="http://localhost:4444/selenium-server/driver/?cmd=shutDow
nSeleniumServer"
      dest="result.txt" ignoreerrors="true" />
  <echo taskname="selenium-shutdown" message="DGF Errors during
shutdown are expected"/>
</target>
```

3. Now that we have that we can now add it to tests so that they are run. This blob calls each of the target items that we created in target. These are in the `antcall` nodes. The `waitForCall` helps us check the Selenium Remote Control server is running before starting the tests:

```
<target name="run_test" description="Start Proxy ; Run Test ;
  stop Proxy">
      <parallel>
```

```
            <antcall target="start-server"></antcall>
            <sequential>
                <echo taskname="waitfor"
                  message="Wait for proxy server launch" />
                <waitfor maxwait="2" maxwaitunit="minute"
                  checkevery="100">
                    <http url="http://localhost:4444/selenium-
server/driver/?cmd=testComplete"/>
                </waitfor>
                    <antcall target="run_test"></antcall>
                    <antcall target="stop-server"></antcall>
            </sequential>
        </parallel>
</target>
```

4. Now we need to tell our CI server to pick this up and run it. On `CruiseControl` we need to add the following XML blob to the `CruiseControl` project file.

```
<schedule>
    <ant antscript="\path\to\ant\batchfile"
         antworkingdir="\path\to\project\"
         buildfile="build.xml"
         uselogger="true"
         usedebug="false"/>
<schedule>
```

What just happened?

We have just created an Ant file that we can use in a continuous integration server to test our tests regularly. Our Ant file started the Selenium Remote Control server and then ran the tests, and once it had completed it shut the Selenium Remote Control server down. The Ant file will look at where the test files have been built and then run them from there.

Summary

We learned a lot in this chapter about using programming languages to drive our Selenium Remote Control tests. Selenium Remote Control can be driven by Java, .NET, Python, Ruby, PHP, and many more languages as they only interact with the proxy.

Specifically, we covered the following topics:

- Converting Selenium IDE tests to a programming language: In this section we had a look at setting up our IDE, we used IDEA for running tests. We then looked at copying our Selenium IDE tests over to a programming language, Java in this case, so we could use Selenium Remote Control in the way it is commonly used.
- Setting up the dependencies: We set up all the dependencies that our tests may need to run and then we started running our tests.
- Writing Selenium tests from scratch: In this section we created the same test as in the previous section as well a few other tests. We did this without using Selenium IDE as a starting point. We saw how we set up our test so that it speaks to a specific Selenium Remote Control and to use a specific browser.
- Selenium Remote Control best practices: In this section we learnt how we can follow some of the major tenets of test automation. We first had a look at how we can always make sure that we start from a known place. We then started refactoring the tests so that all duplicate code was moved into private methods so that we make our tests more maintainable. Finally we had a look at creating tests with the Page Object design pattern. This is a good way to abstract the site under test away from your tests.
- Adding Selenium Remote Control tests to Continuous Integration: In the final section of this chapter we had a look at how we can create an Ant file and have it run by a CI server.

Now that we've learned about creating Selenium Remote Control tests and made them extremely maintainable, we're ready to look at using advanced Selenium calls—which is the topic of the next chapter.

8 Advanced Selenium Techniques

In this chapter we will have a look at how we can do some advanced testing tasks with Selenium. These are all very important items that we need to know so that we can use Selenium to its full potential. We will look at techniques for handling cookies in our tests, working our way to how we do video capture of our tests because a lot of the times our tests will not run on our local development box and we need to see what went wrong.

In this chapter we shall cover the following topics:

- Cookie handling
- Creating new location strategies
- Capturing network traffic with Selenium
- Screen capture while tests are running
- Video capture while tests are running

So let's get on with it...

Important preliminary points

Some of the topics covered in this chapter do not work on 64-Bit Windows. This is not due to Selenium but due to the frameworks that we will be using. It may be beneficial to have an Ubuntu virtual machine ready as a number of the steps can be simplified for that operating system. I will mention when this is needed at the beginning of that section.

Cookie handling

Cookies are a common way to store data between pages, so that as a developer, we do not need to know what is happening on the server other than loading the page. This means that as the person writing the test, we need to know how cookies are handled. For example, doing a negative test by deleting a cookie half-way through the test to validate whether the user loses any information that was stored on the cookie, but that doesn't lock up the browser. Another example is to test that an e-commerce web page is storing the items in a cookie and we need to validate that the items are stored when a new page has loaded. With this in mind let us create a test that gets a single cookie off the page.

Time for action – getting a cookie off the page

Imagine that you are storing the number of times that a page has been visited by a user in a cookie. We then create a test that will load the page and get the cookie by using the `getCookie(name)` call

1. Create a new project in IDEA.
2. Create a new `selenium` instance and then navigate to `/chapter8`.
3. Create a test that then calls `getCookieByName("visitorCount");` where `visitorCount` is the name of the cookie that we need to get.
4. Call `open()` on the page again.
5. Call `getCookieByName("visitorCount");`.
6. Your test code should appear as follows:

```
Selenium selenium;

    @Before
    public void setUp(){
        selenium = new DefaultSelenium("localhost",4444,
          "*chrome","http://book.theautomatedtester.co.uk");
        selenium.start();
    }

    @Test
    public void ShouldGetACookie(){
        selenium.open("/chapter8");
        String cookie = selenium.getCookieByName("visitorCount");
        Assert.assertEquals("Should be 1","1",cookie);
        selenium.open("/chapter8");
        cookie = selenium.getCookieByName("visitorCount");
```

```
        Assert.assertEquals("Should be 2","2",cookie);
    }

    @After
    public void tearDown(){
        selenium.stop();
    }
```

What just happened?

We have just seen how we can get a cookie by specifying the cookie name. We then get a string returned that holds all the information of the cookie. This will be the same as if we needed to interact with the cookie in JavaScript. We can then split the string into its different parts and use it as a key-value store. This makes it extremely useful to test the individual parts and ignore items that contain, dates, for example. But there will be times when we need to get more than one cookie out of the page.

Getting all cookies

Websites store different bits of information in different cookies. This allows web applications to cache different bits of information and then access them as they need. This means that while we are testing these pages we will need to get these items too. We do this by calling `getCookie()`. This will return a string with all cookies and have them separated by a semicolon. This string can then be split on the semicolons to separate the cookies to then do some assertions on the array created from the split.

Time for action – getting all cookies on the page

Let's say that you wanted to add a new cookie for all the items that could be on a list. Since this a way of storing data for different bits of information, getting all the cookies is quite beneficial.

Create a new test and then write Selenium steps to do the following:

1. In the test you will need to load `/chapter8`.
2. Click on the button with the ID `secondCookie`.
3. Get all the cookies on the page with the `getCookie()` call.
4. Validate that there are two cookies returned.
5. Validate that `secondCookie` cookie has the value `anyvalue`.

6. Run the tests.

   Your code should look like the following and should have passed:

```
@Test
public void shouldGetAllCookiesOnThePage(){
    selenium.open("/chapter8");
    selenium.click("secondCookie");
    String[] cookies = selenium.getCookie().split(";");
    Assert.assertEquals(
      "Should be 2 cookies",2,cookies.length);
    Assert.assertEquals("Should be anyvalue",
      "anyvalue",selenium.getCookieByName("secondcookie"));
}
```

What just happened?

We have just seen how we can make one call with Selenium to get all of the cookies on a page. This is useful as we need to add a number of different things to a page to be checked later. We saw how, since the item returned is a string, we can split the string so we can then do a number of different assertions.

Deleting cookies

Part of writing high quality code is being able to test how a page performs when the cookie you expect is not there. You may also want to check that the page doesn't have any residual pieces of information from a previous test that might be there from reusing the browser instance. These two scenarios are by no means the only times that you will want to delete cookies, but they are probably the most common uses.

To delete a cookie we need to call the `deleteCookie` method, passing in two parameters. The first parameter is the name of the cookie, and the second parameter is where it was created. This could be the path or the domain or simply recurse through the cookies until Selenium finds and then deletes it.

Now that we understand what is needed to delete cookies let's see this in action.

Time for action – deleting a cookie

Let's see how we can delete a cookie off the page. In this example we will load the page, delete the cookie, reload the page, and then check the value of the cookie. Use the following steps in your test.

1. Create a new test to work against `http://book.theautomatedtester.co.uk`.

2. Open /chapter8.
3. Delete the cookie. The cookies that are created on that page will be done against path=/. The delete cookie call will appear as follows:

   ```
   selenium.deleteCookie("visitorCount","path=/")
   ```
4. Reload /chapter8.
5. Get the cookie visitorCount and validate that the value is 1.
6. Run your test and check if it passes. Your test should look similar to the following:

   ```
   @Test
   public void shouldDeleteACookieOnThePage(){
       selenium.open("/chapter8");
       selenium.deleteCookie("visitorCount","path=/");
       selenium.open("/chapter8");
       String cookie = selenium.getCookieByName("visitorCount");
       Assert.assertEquals("Should be 1","1",cookie);
   }
   ```

What just happened?

In this section we learned how to delete cookies on the page using Selenium. Selenium has a method—deleteCookie, in which we can pass the name of the cookie that we need to delete, as well as where it has been placed. This call can allow us to control what is stored within the cookies and manipulate them as we need.

We have seen that if we delete the cookie and reload the page the old cookie should not be there, so we can start a different test case.

Pop quiz – working with cookies

- How would you get a cookie by name?
- How would you get all the cookies that are on the page?
- What is returned from getCookie?

Have a go hero – doing more with cookies

Try using the cookie calls against your application if your application works with them. Try getting the cookies and then deleting them and see how your application carries on working after you have done that. In this section you will need to make sure that you use the deleteCookie and getCookie methods to complete this section.

Adding a new location strategy

There are times when we need to find objects on the page that don't involve using the normal techniques for locating elements. We can tell selenium to use a different technique and give it a useful name. For example, if you wanted to have a step that looked like `Selenium.click("foo=bar");` we can use a brand new location strategy without having to recompile Selenium. We do this by calling `addLocationStrategy("name","javascript");`. The JavaScript that we use can access the window and document of the browser by using `inWindow` and `inDocument`. Once the element has been found it needs to return back to Selenium.

For example, we could do:

```
Function(locator){
   Return inDocument.getElementById(locator);
}
```

Let's see this in action

Time for action – adding a new location strategy

In this example we are going to have a look at how we can return the first button on a page.

1. Create a new test.
2. Open `/chapter8`.
3. Add a new location strategy called `firstButton` with the following JavaScript. Use the `addLocatorStrategy` method with the following JavaScript as its parameter:

   ```
   function(nthButton){
     Return inDocument.getElementsByTag("button")[nthButton];
   }
   ```

4. Click on that button using `selenium.click("firstButton=1");`.
5. Run your test. The code should appear as follows:

   ```
   @Test
   Public void shouldCreateANewLocationStrategyAndUseIt(){
     selenium.open("/chapter8");
     selenium.addLocationStrategy("firstButton",
       "function(nthButton){
          return inDocument.getElementsByTag("button")[nthButton];}"
     );
     selenium.click("firstButton=1");
   }
   ```

What just happened?

We have successfully created a new location strategy for looking up elements on the page. We saw how we can create the strategy using the `addLocationStategy` API call into Selenium. This takes two parameters; name of the locator strategy and a JavaScript function that can then do what you want to find the element on the page and then use it. We then can do `foo=bar` where `foo` is the locator strategy and `bar` is the variable passed into the locator strategy function. The location strategy will only last as long as the life of the Selenium instance.

Capturing network traffic

As web applications start to use more and more AJAX to give the look and feel of desktop applications, we start to see that there is a lot of chatter between the web server and the browser. There are times when we need to see what headers are being sent between the web server and the browser so that we can see what is happening if there are errors.

To do this we simply need to change our tests. First we need to pass in a parameter `captureNetworkTraffic=true` when we start the browser and then when we need the data we just call `captureNetworkTraffic` with a parameter of how we would like the results returned. This can be a plain, JSON, or XML. Let's now see this in action.

Time for action – capturing network traffic

Let's say that you want to capture the network traffic and assert that something is being cached properly. To do this we will add the new parameter to start and then capture it after the page has loaded.

1. Create a new test.
2. Change the browser start code if you have it in the `@Before` to appear as follows:

   ```
   Selenium.start("captureNetworkTraffic=true")
   ```

3. Open `/chapter8`.
4. Call `captureNetworkTraffic` with either plain, JSON, or XML. I have called it with JSON as it's easy to serialize into a dictionary for testing. You can call it with XML or plain as the parameters.
5. Print the result to the console

6. Run your test. The code should appear as follows:

```
@Test
public void shouldCaptureNetworkTraffic(){
    selenium.open("/chapter8");
    String json = selenium.captureNetworkTraffic("JSON");
    System.out.println(json);
}
```

The output should look something like this:


```
[{
    statusCode: 403,
    method: 'GET',
    url: 'http://localhost:4444/favicon.ico',
    bytes: 1244,
    start: '2010-06-27T10:30:28.609-0700',
    end: '2010-06-27T10:30:28.868-0700',
    timeInMillis: 259,
    requestHeaders:[{
        name: 'Host',
        value: 'localhost:4444'
    },{
        name: 'User-Agent',
        value: 'Mozilla/5.0 (X11; U; Linux i686; en-US; rv:1.9.2.3)
          Gecko/20100423 Ubuntu/10.04 (lucid) Firefox/3.6.3'
    },{
        name: 'Accept',
        value: 'image/png,image/*;q=0.8,*/*;q=0.5'
    },{
        name: 'Accept-Language',
        value: 'en-us,en;q=0.5'
    },{
        name: 'Accept-Encoding',
        value: 'gzip,deflate'
    },{
        name: 'Accept-Charset',
        value: 'ISO-8859-1,utf-8;q=0.7,*;q=0.7'
    },{
        name: 'keep-alive',
        value: '115'
```

What just happened?

We have just seen how we can store the network traffic that is happening between the browser and the web server serving the pages that Selenium requests. The results can either be in a plain text mode, JSON or XML. Selenium will return a string that we can then easily load into the different data types.

Once we have manipulated the results we can then have a look at what is in what is returned and do assertions on it.

Now that we have captured the traffic between Selenium and the web server, let's have a look at capturing screenshots.

Capturing screenshots

A lot of the time our Selenium Remote control browsers will be running on machines that differ from the machine that started the tests. As a developer or tester, you need a mechanism in place to have a screenshot of what the error looks like when a test fails, preferably images that are captured in the PNG format.

Unfortunately capturing screenshots in Selenium is limited to Mozilla Firefox and Internet Explorer. This is due to these browsers having libraries that Selenium can use to take screenshots. As more libraries are added to Selenium for different browsers you will be able to take more screenshots. They will use the same API call so there will be no need for you to change your tests.

captureScreenshot call

The first call that we are going to have a look at is the `captureScreenshot` call. This will take a screenshot of the entire screen and not just the browser. This is extremely useful to see what is happening on the desktop when the test fails and it could be something outside of the browser.

We call `captureScreenshot(file)` where `file` is path and file name of the file that you want to save. If you give it just the filename it will save the file in the same folder as Selenium Remote Control server, or if you pass in the absolute path of the file it will save it to where you want it to go. Let's see this in action.

Time for action – capturing screenshots

Let's say that you have a situation where you need to capture a screenshot on failure or just capture screenshots for a user manual. Let's write a test to take such a screenshot.

1. Create a new test.
2. Load `chapter8`.
3. Take a screenshot and save it somewhere where you can access it.
4. Run the test. Your code should appear as follows:

```
@Test
public void shouldTakeAScreenShot(){
    selenium.open("/chapter8");
    selenium.captureScreenshot("003.png");
}
```

5. This should take a screenshot similar to the following:

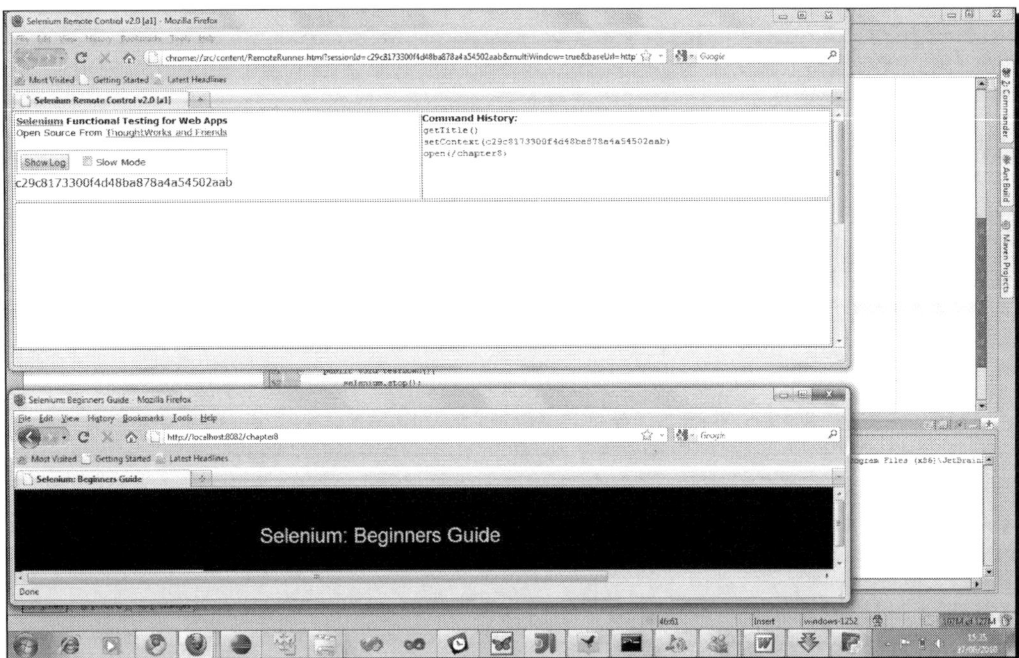

What just happened?

We have just seen how we can use Selenium to capture a screenshot of what is happening on the page. We saw how `captureScreenshot` captures an image of the entire desktop. This can be extremely useful to see what is currently running on the desktop when it does fail, if that is useful.

We can also store the result of capture screen shot into a `base64` encoded string using Selenium. This could be due to the need to make changes to what is returned and then write it to disk. A example of this is Michael Tamm's CSS layout bug framework.

Let's see this in action.

Time for action – capturing a screenshot to string

Let's say that we wanted to manipulate the screenshots before they are written to the disk, or you didn't want to save the images on the same machine that the Selenium RC is running on; we would need a mechanism to do so. For that we would use `captureScreenshotToString()`.

1. Create a new test.
2. Open `/chapter8`.
3. Call `captureScreenshotToString()`.
4. Print the result of the previous step to the console.
5. Run your tests. Your code should look similar to the following:

```
@Test
public void shouldTakeAScreenshotAndReturnAScreenshot(){
    selenium.open("/chapter8");
    String screenshot = selenium.captureScreenshotToString();
    System.out.println(screenshot);
}
```

What just happened?

We have just seen how we can take a screenshot and the result is passed back as the string. This can be then used to do a number of things within your test such as comparing two screenshots to see if anything has changed.

Capturing the entire page

In the previous section we saw how you can take a screenshot of the desktop by using the `captureScreenshot` method call. However, there is one downside to using that call. The image that is written to the disk does not have the screenshot of the entire page that we are testing. Seeing a screenshot of the entire page is extremely useful when having to debug issues on a page that have been flagged up by Selenium.

Selenium does this using a method called `captureEntirePageScreenshot` and passes in two parameters. The first parameter is where the file is to be saved. The second parameter is for when you need to change the background of the HTML. This could be because there may be an issue with the color of the text on the background. Changing the background makes it clearer in the screenshot. We will next see examples of both next.

Time for action – capturing the entire page as a screenshot

Imagine that you are working against a web page that is longer than your physical desktop. As a user, you would scroll down to that item to see it but unfortunately Selenium doesn't do this.

To do this we will call:

```
captureEntirePageScreenshot("path/to/save/file.png","");
```

1. Create a new test.
2. Get the test to open `/chapter8`.
3. Create a screenshot of that page and save it locally.
4. Run the test. The code should produce an image similar to the following:

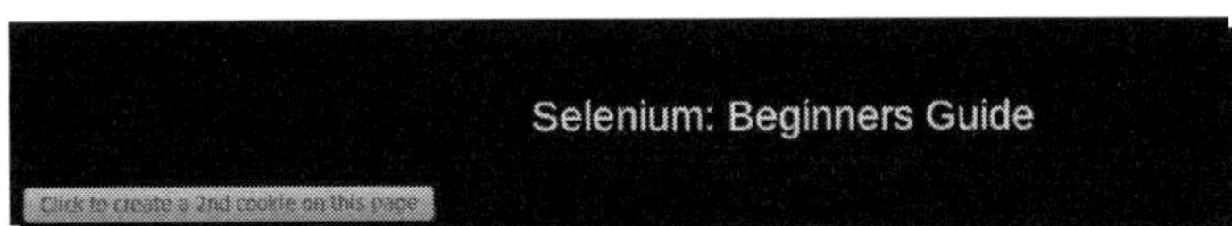

Your code should appear as follows. This is saving it to somewhere on my linux VM.

```
public void shouldTakeAScreenShotEntirePage(){
    selenium.open("/chapter8");
    selenium.captureEntirePageScreenshot(
      "/home/automatedtester/entirepage.png","");
}
```

What just happened?

We have just taken a screenshot of what is inside the browser and not the entire desktop. This could be due to the fact that we want to take a screenshot of the page when it is longer than the desktop. We call `captureEntirePageScreenshot` with the parameter for where we want the image to be saved and then an empty parameter.

There are times where we will need to take a screenshot of the page and change the background of the body tag. This is to try to help us diagnose any CSS issues, especially for browsers on operating systems that you are not developing against. To change the background we need to change the empty parameter in the previous example to `background=hexcolour`. Let's see this in action now.

Time for action – capture entire page as a screenshot changing background colour

Imagine that you need to change the background to see any potential issues with CSS. To do this we are going to call:

```
captureEntirePageScreenshot(
  "/path/to/file.png","background=#ccffdd"
);
```

This will change the background to a pale green.

1. Create a new test.
2. Get the test to open `/chapter8`.
3. Capture the entire page.
4. Run your test. It should take a screenshot similar to the following:

And the test should appear as follows:

```
@Test
public void shouldTakeAScreenShotEntirePageChangingBackground()
{
     selenium.open("/chapter8");
     selenium.captureEntirePageScreenshot(
       "/home/automatedtester/entirepagediffbackground.png",
       "background=#CCFFDD");
}
```

What just happened?

We have just seen how we can take a screenshot of the page and then change the background so that we can capture any potential CSS issues that are on the screen.

As with `captureScreenshot` we can call a different method to have it return a `Base64` string that we can use. This means that we can do manipulations or just write it to a folder where the tests are being run rather than on the server with Selenium Remote Control.

Time for action – capturing the entire page screenshot to a string

As in `captureScreenshot` there are a number of different reasons why we may want to have the screenshot returned to us as a string. In this example we will be calling `captureEntirePageScreenshotToString(parameter);`. `parameter` takes the same as the second parameter we saw in `captureEntirePageScreenshot`.

1. Create a new test.
2. Get selenium to open `/chapter8`.
3. Call `captureEntirePageScreenshotToString("");` and store the result in a string.
4. Print the string to the console.
5. Run your test. Your test should appear as follows:

```
@Test
public void
shouldTakeAScreenShotEntirePageAndReturnABase64String(){
    selenium.open("/chapter8");
    String screenshot = selenium.
captureEntirePageScreenshotToString("");
    System.out.println(screenshot);
}
```

What just happened?

We have just seen how we can take screenshots of the entire HTML and then return it as a string. We can pass a keyworded argument that can pass in early if we wanted to change the background for the body.

Capturing screenshots is useful but if you can capture video, that would be exciting.

Pop quiz

- What is the default file type for capturing screenshots?
- How does one capture a screenshot of the entire desktop?
- When capturing shots to string, how is the string encoded?

Have a go hero

Capturing screenshots is extremely useful when something goes wrong, and this can sometimes be used to find major CSS issues on a page. Try and create a test that finds out when text has overflowed in a textbox. For this you will need to create a test to change the text color to white, and the borders of boxes to a strong color, and then take a screenshot. Then do the same except changing the text to black and take a screenshot. Now take the two screenshots and compare them.

Capturing video

They say a picture is worth a thousand words, so a video must be priceless, especially a video of a test. One of the main Selenium-based companies uses a framework called Castro as a mechanism for creating videos while the tests are running. Castro is a video framework that uses VNC to view what is on the desktop and then stores the data in a file that can be viewed from a web application. Let's start by setting up the environment. I suggest using an Ubuntu VM for this section of the book.

Time for action – setting up the environment to capture video

For setting up VNC, use the following steps:

1. Go to **System | Preferences | Remote Desktop Preferences**.
2. Check **Allow others to view your desktop**.
3. Now that we have VNC setup we will need to install a few libraries that our video capture rely on. Since we are using Ubuntu it is a simple case on

   ```
   sudo apt-get install python-dev python-pygame python-tk python-setuptools ffmpeg flvtool2
   ```

4. Now we need to install Castro. We do this by running `sudo easy_install castro`.

What just happened?

We have successfully installed all the tools that we need to start recording with Castro. If you want to record on other platforms you can use the Python setup tools to download and install the items that I have listed there.

Now that we have everything set up, let's create our first video.

Time for action – recording a video in a test

In this *Time for action* we are going to be using Python to do this test. You can write your tests in Java and call into Castro with Jython if need be.

We start by creating a new video object for Castro in the setup, passing in the name of the file that we want it to be saved as. We then start up the video recording in the same manner as Selenium, by calling `start()`.

Once the test has finished running we then call `stop()` on that object to stop recording. Once that call has finished we call `process()` to apply the correct encoding to the video. We can see an example of that next:

1. Create a new test file and put the following in there.

```
from selenium import selenium
import unittest, time, re, castro

class VideoRecord(unittest.TestCase):
    def setUp(self):
        self.verificationErrors = []
        self.video = castro.Castro(filename="filename.flv")
        self.video.start()
        self.selenium = selenium("localhost",
          4444, "*firefox",
          "http://www.theautomatedtester.co.uk/")
        self.selenium.start()
        self.selenium.window_maximize()

    def test_my(self):
      sel = self.selenium
      sel.open("/")
      sel.click("link=blog")
      sel.wait_for_page_to_load("30000")

    def tearDown(self):
        self.selenium.stop()
```

```
            self.video.stop()
            self.video.process()
            self.assertEqual([], self.verificationErrors)

    if __name__ == "__main__":
        unittest.main()
```

What just happened?

We have created a new Castro object passing in the name of the file that we want to have it saved to. By passing in a file name we can tell it to use the FLV which can then be uploaded to sites such as YouTube and Vimeo

In the teardown we saw how we stop the video and then we call `process()`. The process call will take the image and then apply all the correct encodings to the page.

Pop quiz

- What is the name of the library we used to record video?
- What is the desktop viewing application Castro relies on?

Have a go hero

Try getting this set up on a Windows machine. To do this you will need to install a Windows VNC client like TightVNC or RealVNC. The rest of the steps for setting up Castro should be the same.

Summary

We learned a lot in this chapter about the advanced things that we can do with Selenium.

Specifically, we covered the following topics:

- **Cookie Handling**: In this section we had a look at how we can use Selenium to get cookies on the page so that we can validate the data that they store. We then saw how we can get all the cookies that are on the page. The `getCookie()` call returns all the cookies on the page as a string that is delimited by a semicolon. Finally in this section we had a look at how we can delete cookies while the tests are running.
- **Adding location strategies**: In this section we had a look at how we can create our own location strategies by telling Selenium to use a JavaScript function we pass it with the `addLocationStrategy("strategyName","search method");`.

- **Capturing network traffic**: In this section we had a look at how we can capture the network traffic that is happening between the browser and the web server. Selenium Remote Control server captures all the information and then when we call `captureNetworkTraffic("JSON")` we get the information back in JSON. We can also use plain and XML as the type.
- **Capturing screenshots**: We had a look at how we can get Selenium to take a screenshot of the entire desktop to see if there is anything there. This uses the `captureScreenshot` call but if we needed the screenshot returned to the test as a string we can call `captureScreenshotToString()` to get a `Base64` encoded string.
- **Capturing video**: Capturing video of tests while they are running allows us to get a lot more value out of issues when they go wrong. We saw how using another library in our tests can be of great value and in this case allowed us to create videos of our tests while they are running.

Now that we've learned about all the advanced things we can do with Selenium, we're ready to have a look at Selenium Grid—which is the topic of the next chapter.

9

Getting Started with Selenium Grid

In this chapter we are going to have a look at what Selenium Grid is and how we can set it up in different environments, including how to set it up on Amazon EC2. This will abstract the topography of where the tests are located so that your tests only have to worry about one address.

In this chapter we shall cover the following topics:

- Setting up the Selenium Grid Hub
- Setting up the Selenium Grid Remote Controls
- Creating tests for the Grid

So let's get on with it...

Important preliminary points

For this section you will need to have Apache Ant on the machine that you are going to have running Grid instances. You can get this from `http://ant.apache.org/bindownload.cgi` for Windows and Mac. If you have Ubuntu you can simply do `sudo apt-get install ant1.8`, which will install all the relevant items that are needed onto your Linux machine. You will also have to download the latest Selenium Grid from `http://selenium-grid.seleniumhq.org/download.html`.

Understanding Selenium Grid

Selenium Grid is a version of Selenium that allows teams to set up a number of Selenium instances and then have one central point to send your Selenium commands to. This differs from what we saw in Selenium Remote Control (RC) where we always had to explicitly say where the Selenium RC is as well as know what browsers that Remote Control can handle.

With Selenium Grid, we just ask for a specific browser, and then the hub that is part of Selenium Grid will route all the Selenium commands through to the Remote Control you want.

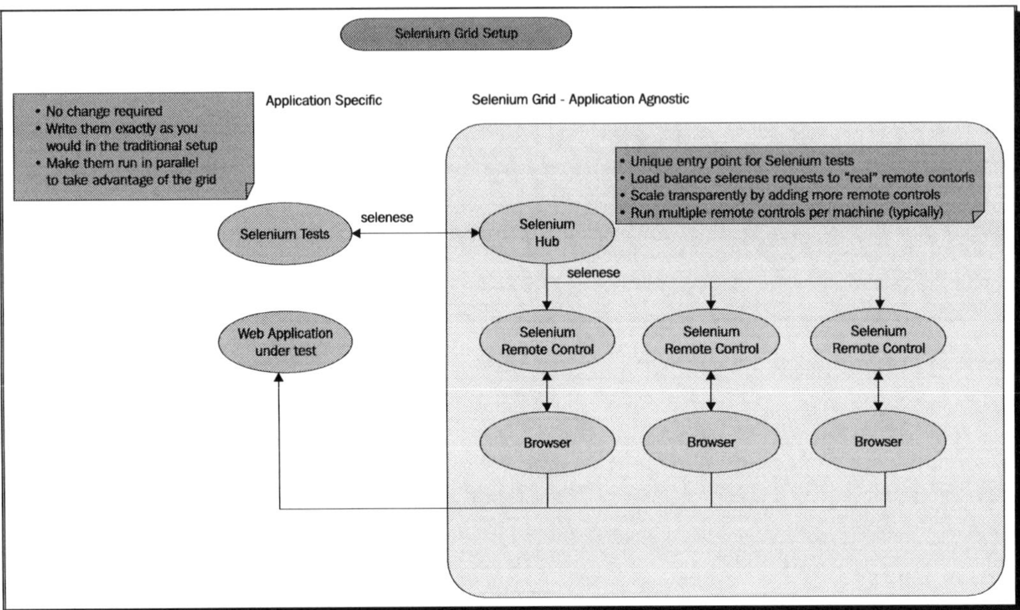

Selenium Grid also allows us to, with the help of the configuration file, assign friendly names to the Selenium RC instances so that when the tests want to run against Firefox on Linux, the hub will find a free instance and then route all the Selenium Commands from your test through to the instance that is registered with that environment. We can see an example of this in the next diagram.

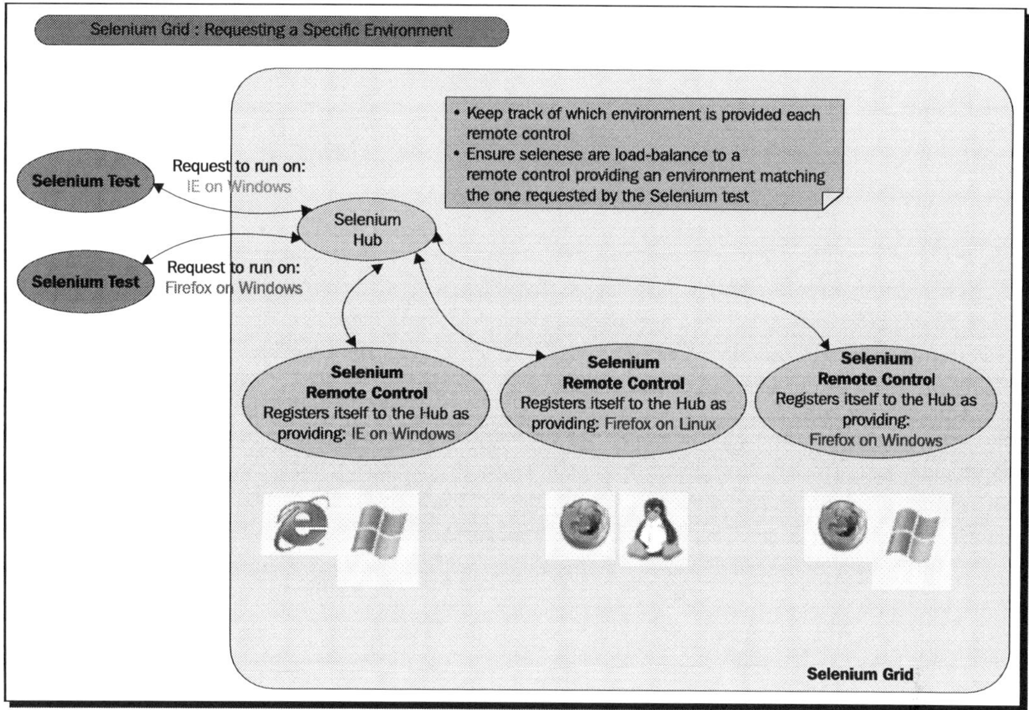

We will see how to create tests for this later in the chapter, but for now let's have a look at making sure we have all the necessary items ready for the grid.

Checking that we have the necessary items for Selenium Grid

Now that you have downloaded Selenium Grid and Ant, it is always good to run a sanity check on Selenium Grid to make sure that we are ready to go. To do this we run a simple command in a console or Command Prompt.

Let's see this in action.

Time for action – doing a sanity check on Selenium Grid

1. Open a Command Prompt or console window.
2. Run the command `ant sanity-check`. When it is complete you should see something similar to the next screenshot:

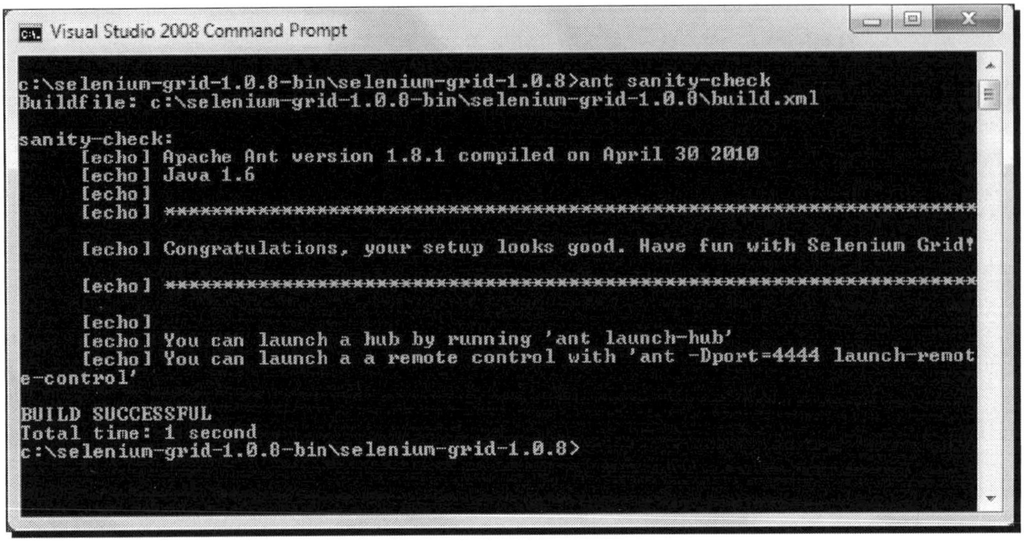

```
Visual Studio 2008 Command Prompt

c:\selenium-grid-1.0.8-bin\selenium-grid-1.0.8>ant sanity-check
Buildfile: c:\selenium-grid-1.0.8-bin\selenium-grid-1.0.8\build.xml

sanity-check:
     [echo] Apache Ant version 1.8.1 compiled on April 30 2010
     [echo] Java 1.6
     [echo]
     [echo] ***************************************************************

     [echo] Congratulations, your setup looks good. Have fun with Selenium Grid!

     [echo] ***************************************************************

     [echo]
     [echo] You can launch a hub by running 'ant launch-hub'
     [echo] You can launch a a remote control with 'ant -Dport=4444 launch-remot
e-control'

BUILD SUCCESSFUL
Total time: 1 second
c:\selenium-grid-1.0.8-bin\selenium-grid-1.0.8>
```

What just happened?

We have just checked whether we have all the necessary items to run Selenium Grid. If there was something that Selenium relied on, the sanity check script would output what was needed so that you could easily correct this. Now that everything is ready, let us start setting up the Grid.

Selenium Grid Hub

Selenium Grid works by having a central point that tests can connect to, and commands are then pushed to the Selenium Remote Control instances connected to that hub. The hub has a web interface that tells you about the Selenium Remote Control instances that are connected to the Hub, and whether they are currently in use.

Time for action – launching the hub

Now that we are ready to start working with Selenium Grid we need to set up the Grid. This is a simple command that we run in the console or Command Prompt.

1. Open a Command Prompt or console window.
2. Run the command `ant launch-hub`. When that happens you should see something similar to the following screenshot:

```
automatedtester@ubuntu:~/Downloads/selenium-grid-1.0.8$ ant launch-hub
Buildfile: /home/automatedtester/Downloads/selenium-grid-1.0.8/build.xml

launch-hub:
     [java] Jul 11, 2010 8:07:24 PM com.thoughtworks.selenium.grid.hub.HubRegist
ry gridConfiguration
     [java] INFO: Loaded grid configuration:
     [java] ---
     [java] hub:
     [java]   environments:
     [java]     -
     [java]       browser: "*firefox"
     [java]       name: Firefox on Windows
     [java]     -
     [java]       browser: "*firefox"
     [java]       name: Firefox on OS X
     [java]     -
     [java]       browser: "*firefox"
     [java]       name: Firefox on Linux
     [java]     -
     [java]       browser: "*iehta"
     [java]       name: IE on Windows
     [java]     -
     [java]       browser: "*safari"
```

We can see that this is running in the command prompt or console. We can also see the hub running from within a browser.

If we put `http://nameofmachine:4444/console` where `nameofmachine` is the name of the machine with the hub. If it is on your machine then you can place `http://localhost:4444/console`. We can see that in the next screenshot:

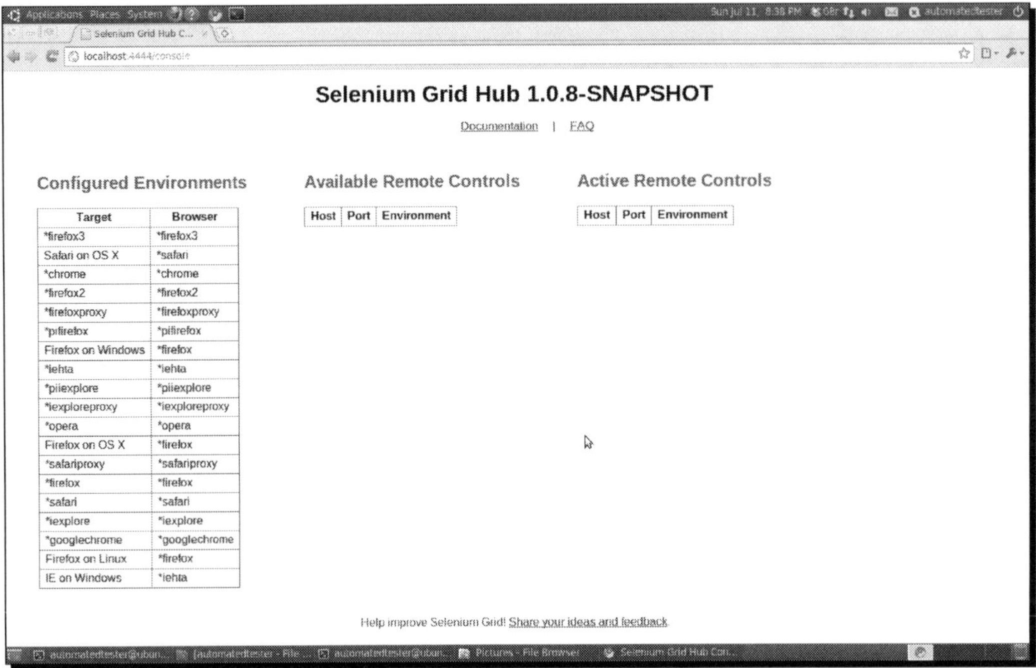

What just happened?

We have successfully started Selenium Grid Hub. This is the central point of our tests and Selenium Grid instances. We saw that when we start Selenium Grid it showed us what items were available according to the configuration file that is with the normal install.

We then had a look at how we can see what the Grid is doing by having a look at the hub in a browser. We did this by putting the URL `http://nameofmachine:4444/console` where `nameofmachine` is the name of the machine that we would like to access with the hub. It shows what configured environments the hub can handle, what grid instances are available and which instances are currently active.

Now that we have the hub ready we can have a look at starting up instances.

Adding instances to the hub

Now that we have successfully started the Selenium Grid Hub, we will need to have a look at how we can start adding Selenium Remote Controls to the hub so that it starts forming the grid of computers that we are expecting. As with everything in Selenium Grid, we need Ant to start the instances that connect. In the next few *Time for action* sections we will see the different arguments needed to start instances to join the grid.

Time for action – adding a remote control with the defaults

In this section we are going to launch Selenium Remote Control and get it to register with the hub. We are going to assume that the browser you would like it to register for is Firefox, and the hub is on the same machine as the Remote Control. We will pass in only one required argument, which is the port that we wish it to run on. However, when starting instances, we will always need to pass in the port since Selenium cannot work out if there are any free ports on the host machine.

1. Open a Command Prompt or console window.
2. Enter the command `ant -Dport=5555 launch-remote-control` and press *Return*. You should see the following in your Command Prompt or console:

```
automatedtester@ubuntu: ~/Downloads/selenium-grid-1.0.8
File Edit View Terminal Help
automatedtester@ubuntu:~/Downloads/selenium-grid-1.0.8$ ant -Dport=5555 launch-r
emote-control
Buildfile: /home/automatedtester/Downloads/selenium-grid-1.0.8/build.xml

launch-remote-control:
     [java] Jul 11, 2010 10:24:14 PM com.thoughtworks.selenium.grid.remotecontro
l.RegistrationRequest execute
     [java] INFO: Registering to http://localhost:4444/registration-manager/regi
ster
     [java] Jul 11, 2010 10:24:15 PM com.thoughtworks.selenium.grid.remotecontro
l.SelfRegisteringRemoteControl logStartingMessages
     [java] INFO: Starting selenium server with options:[RegistrationInfo seleni
umHubURL='http://localhost:4444', env='*firefox', host='localhost', port='5555']
     [java] Jul 11, 2010 10:24:15 PM com.thoughtworks.selenium.grid.remotecontro
l.SelfRegisteringRemoteControl logStartingMessages
     [java] INFO: hubPollerInterval: 30000 ms
     [java] Jul 11, 2010 10:24:15 PM com.thoughtworks.selenium.grid.remotecontro
l.SelfRegisteringRemoteControl logStartingMessages
     [java] INFO: -port
     [java] Jul 11, 2010 10:24:15 PM com.thoughtworks.selenium.grid.remotecontro
l.SelfRegisteringRemoteControl logStartingMessages
     [java] INFO: 5555
     [java] 22:24:15.437 INFO - Java: Sun Microsystems Inc. 14.0-b16
     [java] 22:24:15.472 INFO - OS: Linux 2.6.32-23-generic i386
```

And this in the Selenium Grid Hub site:

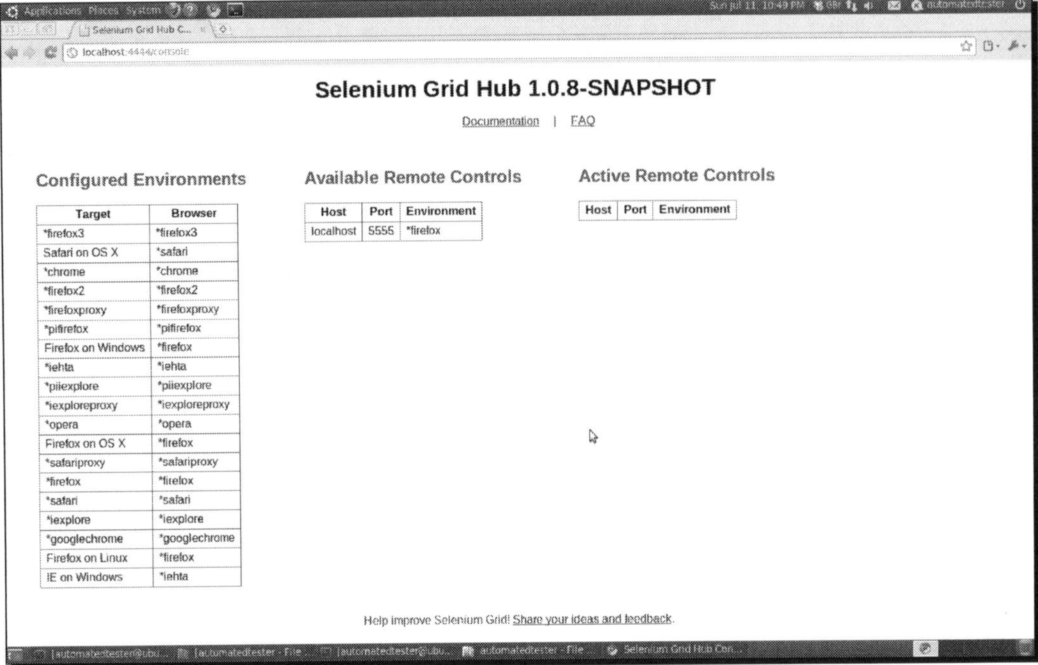

What just happened?

We have added the first machine to our own Selenium Grid. It has used all the defaults that are in the Ant build script and it has created a Selenium Remote Control that will take any Firefox requests, located on the same machine as the host of Selenium Remote Control Grid. This is a useful way to set up the grid if you just want a large number of Firefox-controlling Selenium Remote Controls.

Adding Selenium Remote Controls for different machines

Selenium Grid is most powerful when you can add it to multiple operating systems. This allows us to check, for instance, whether Firefox on Windows and Firefox on Linux is doing the same thing during a test. To register new remote controls to the grid from a machine other than the one hosting the hub, we need to tell it where the hub is. We do this by passing in the `-DhubURL` argument when calling the Ant script. We also need to pass in the `-Dhost` argument with the name of the machine so that we can see where it is being hosted.

Let's see this in action.

Time for action – adding Selenium Remote Controls for different machines

For this *Time for action* you will need to have another machine available for you to use. This could be the Ubuntu machine that you needed for the previous chapter. I suggest giving the `-Dhost` argument the name of the machine that it is running on. If you have a small Grid then you can name them according to the operating system that it is run on.

1. Open a Command Prompt or console.
2. Run the command `ant -Dport=9999 -DhubURL=http://nameofmachine:port -Dhost=nameofcurrentmachine launch-remote-control`.
3. When you have run this, your Grid site should appear as follows:

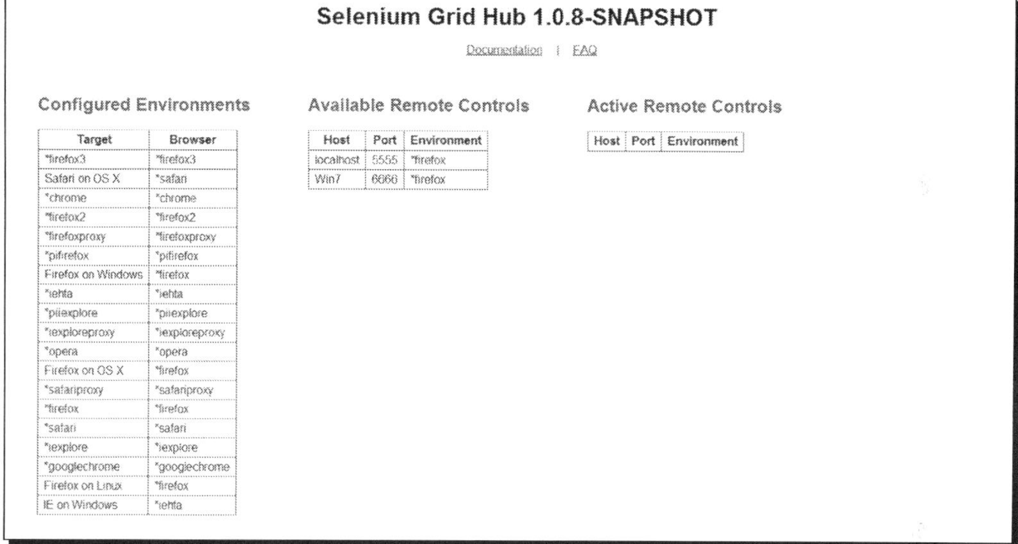

What just happened?

We have added a new remote control to the grid from a machine other than where the Selenium Grid Hub is running. This is the first time that we have been able to set up our remote control instances in a grid. We learnt about the `-DhubURL` argument and the `-Dhost` argument that is needed when launching the remote control. We then saw that it has updated the Grid site that is running on the hub.

Now that we have this working as we expect, let us have a look at setting up browsers other than Firefox.

Adding Selenium Remote Control for different browsers

Selenium Grid is extremely powerful when we start using different browsers on the grid, since we can't run all the different browsers on a single machine due to operating systems and browser combinations. There are currently up to nine different combinations that are used by most people, so getting Selenium Grid to help with this can give you the test coverage that you need. To do this we pass in the `-Denvironment` argument in our Ant call. The value that we assign to this has to be Selenium Grid configuration. The Selenium Grid configuration comes with a number of preset items. This is visible from the Selenium Grid Hub page that we have seen already. Let us now see how we can set the items.

Time for action – setting the Environment when starting Selenium Remote Control

Now that we need to get Internet Explorer Selenium Remote controls added to our grid. We have to add the `-Denvironment` argument to our call with the target on the configured environments. Since we want an Internet Explorer remote control we can use the IE on Windows targets.

1. Open a console or Command Prompt window.
2. Run the command `ant -Dport=9998 -DhubURL=addressofhub -Dhost=nameofremotehost -Denvironment="IE on Windows" launch-remote-control`.
3. When it is running, your hub page should appear as follows:

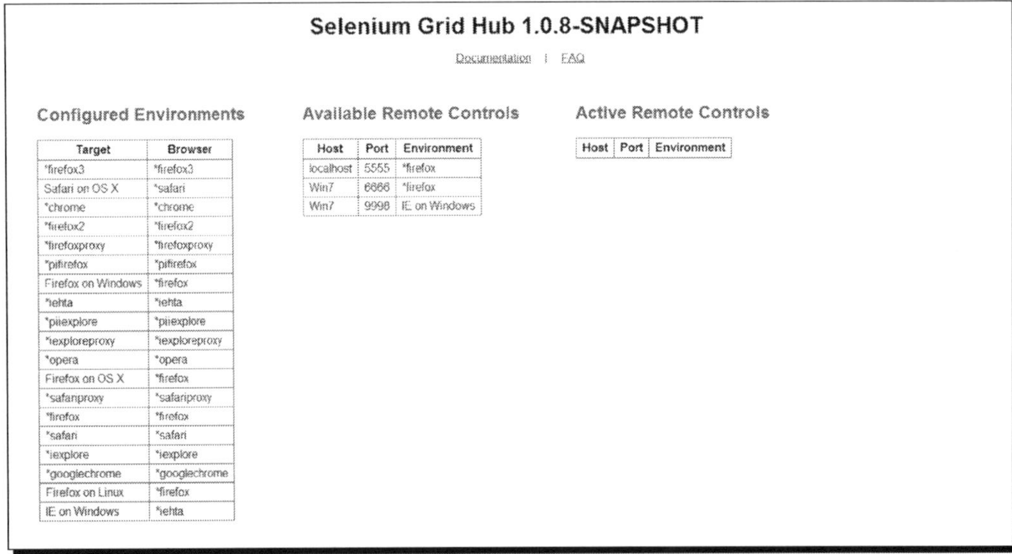

Selenium Grid Hub 1.0.8-SNAPSHOT

Documentation | FAQ

Configured Environments

Target	Browser
*firefox3	*firefox3
Safari on OS X	*safari
*chrome	*chrome
*firefox2	*firefox2
*firefoxproxy	*firefoxproxy
*pifirefox	*pifirefox
Firefox on Windows	*firefox
*iehta	*iehta
*piiexplore	*piiexplore
*iexploreproxy	*iexploreproxy
*opera	*opera
Firefox on OS X	*firefox
*safariproxy	*safariproxy
*firefox	*firefox
*safari	*safari
*iexplore	*iexplore
*googlechrome	*googlechrome
Firefox on Linux	*firefox
IE on Windows	*iehta

Available Remote Controls

Host	Port	Environment
localhost	5555	*firefox
Win7	6666	*firefox
Win7	9998	IE on Windows

Active Remote Controls

Host	Port	Environment

What just happened?

We have just seen how we can create more verbose environment names such as "IE on Windows". We also saw how we can start a remote control for different browsers. This is quite useful when we need to test a large amount of browser and operating system combinations.

Updating the Selenium Grid Configuration

The Configured Environments come with a standard installation but there are times where it would be useful to set up your own targets. This could be when browsers that used to work on a specific operating system now work on multiple operating systems. We have already seen this happen with Google Chrome.

To update the configuration we need to have a look at the `grid_configuration.yml`. This is a YAML file that contains all the configurations that Selenium grid has. We need to add a new name and browser for new items. For example:

```
-name:  "Google Chrome on Windows"
 Browser: "*googlechrome"
```

Let's see this in action.

Time for action – adding new items to the Grid Configuration

As we saw from the default configuration that is distributed, it doesn't have the different flavors of Google Chrome. We can add this to the file this time so we can extend the coverage that we need.

1. Open `grid_configuration.yml` in a text editor.

   Add the following to the file:

   ```
   -name:  "Google Chrome on Windows"
    Browser: "*googlechrome"
   ```

2. Start the hub.

3. In another console or Command Prompt, run the newly created item. While running, your Grid should appear as follows:

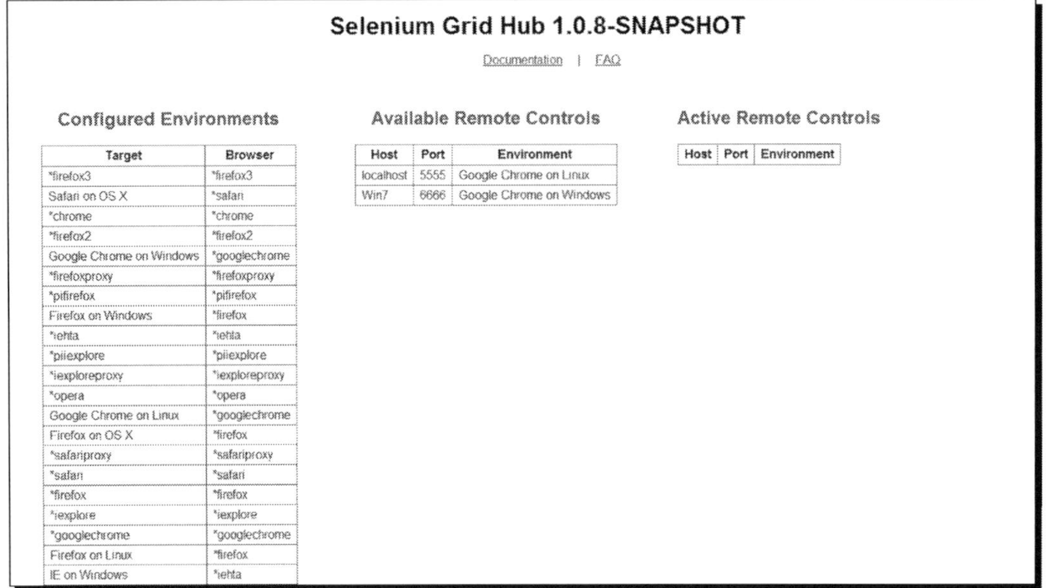

Selenium Grid Hub 1.0.8-SNAPSHOT

Documentation | FAQ

Configured Environments

Target	Browser
*firefox3	*firefox3
Safari on OS X	*safari
*chrome	*chrome
*firefox2	*firefox2
Google Chrome on Windows	*googlechrome
*firefoxproxy	*firefoxproxy
*pifirefox	*pifirefox
Firefox on Windows	*firefox
*iehta	*iehta
*piiexplore	*piiexplore
*iexploreproxy	*iexploreproxy
*opera	*opera
Google Chrome on Linux	*googlechrome
Firefox on OS X	*firefox
*safariproxy	*safariproxy
*safari	*safari
*firefox	*firefox
*iexplore	*iexplore
*googlechrome	*googlechrome
Firefox on Linux	*firefox
IE on Windows	*iehta

Available Remote Controls

Host	Port	Environment
localhost	5555	Google Chrome on Linux
Win7	6666	Google Chrome on Windows

Active Remote Controls

Host	Port	Environment

What just happened?

We have just added our first item to the Grid Configuration. This could be renaming an item so that it makes a lot more sense, or if there is something missing that is needed. We can give each of the items meaningful names that then point to a specific browser. We can also use this to set up custom browsers if need be.

Pop quiz – doing the thing

- What is the command required to start the Hub?
- What is the URL where one can see what is happening on the Grid?
- How do you specify the port that the Remote Control is running on?
- How do you specify which browser you would like the Remote Control to be registered with?

Running tests against the Grid

Now that we have set up the Grid with different instances, we should have a look at how we can write tests against these Remote Controls on the Grid. We can pass in the value of the target that we can see in the grid and then run the tests. So instead of passing in `*firefox` you can use "firefox on linux" and then run the tests as usual.

Let's see this in action.

Time for action – writing tests against the grid

1. Create a new test file.
2. Populate it with a test script that accesses an item on the grid and then works against `http://book.theautomatedtester.co.uk/`. Your script should look similar to the following:

```
import org.junit.*;
import com.thoughtworks.selenium.*;

public class TestExamples2 {

    Selenium selenium;

    @Before
    public void setUp(){
        selenium = new DefaultSelenium("192.168.157.153",4444,
          "Google Chrome on Linux",
          "http://book.theautomatedtester.co.uk");//
        selenium.start();
    }

    @After
    public void tearDown(){
        selenium.stop();
    }

    @Test
    public void ShouldRunTestsAgainstGoogleChromeOnLinux(){
        selenium.open("/");
        selenium.click("link=chapter2");
    }
}
```

What just happened?

We have just seen how we can write tests that can run against the Grid and then run them. When the tests are running the grid will show which Remote Control is currently in use and which grid items are currently free. We can see this in the following screenshot:

Selenium Grid Hub 1.0.8-SNAPSHOT

Documentation | FAQ

Configured Environments

Target	Browser
*firefox3	*firefox3
Safari on OS X	*safari
*chrome	*chrome
*firefox2	*firefox2
Google Chrome on Windows	*googlechrome
*firefoxproxy	*firefoxproxy
*pifirefox	*pifirefox

Available Remote Controls

Host	Port	Environment
Win7	6666	Google Chrome on Windows

Active Remote Controls

Host	Port	Environment
localhost	5555	Google Chrome on Linux

Summary

We learned a lot in this chapter about how to set up Selenium Grid and all the different arguments needed, as well as running our tests against the Grid.

Specifically, we covered:

- **Starting Selenium Grid Hub**: In this section of the book we had a look at how we can start up Selenium Grid Hub that is the central point for Selenium Grid.
- **Setting up Selenium Grid Remote Controls**: We had a look at all the arguments that are needed to add a Remote Control to the Grid so that we can use it. This gives us a more manageable view of our grid so that we can work with it.

We also discussed how we can create tests that use the grid.

Now that we've learned about setting up Selenium Grid, we're ready to look into getting our test time down by running things in parallel using Selenium Grid—which is the topic of the next chapter.

10

Running Selenium Tests in Parallel

In this chapter we will have a look at how to create tests that run in parallel using Selenium Grid. Using Selenium Grid in this fashion we can develop tests that run a lot faster.

Traditionally Selenium tests run sequentially in the order that our test framework decides.

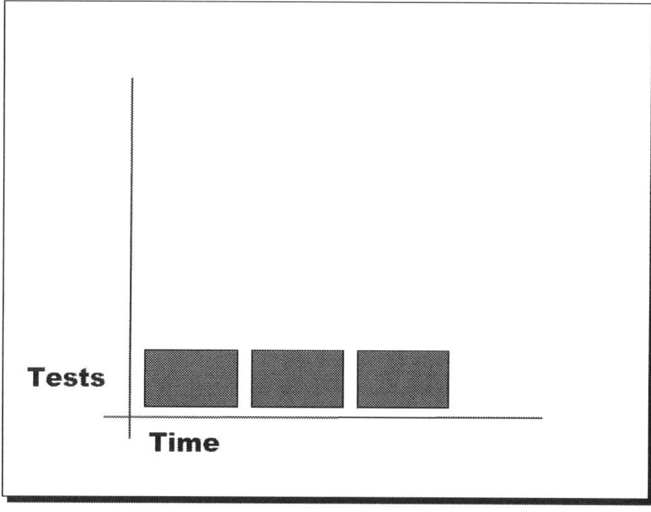

We can now run our test in parallel, meaning we start running tests in `1/n`th the time, where `n` is the number of browsers that we want to test with, as we can see in the following graph:

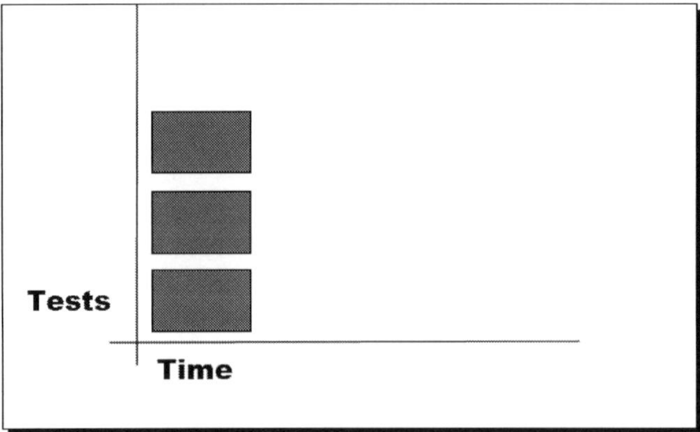

In this chapter we shall cover the following activities:

- Setting up TestNG
- Running a test
- Running multiple tests

So let's get on with it...

Important preliminary points

In this chapter we need to use a testing framework that supports parallel running of our tests. I recommend using TestNG from `http://testng.org` to run our tests. TestNG uses an XML configuration client that fires up multiple threads and runs the tests as we need them. It does, however, use the same annotations that our JUnit tests used in previous chapters.

If you are using Python you can use Nose, pNunit if you are using .NET, or DeepTest if you are using Ruby.

Setting up TestNG

TestNG is a popular testing framework that allows us to create tests that then can be run in parallel. We can set up test suites and have parameters that we need placed in there. Let's start by creating a test suite.

Time for action – starting to create the test suite

TestNG requires that we have an XML configuration file that it can look at before the tests begin. This means that we can control how our tests are run when we need to run them.

1. Create a new XML file in a text editor and call it `testng.xml`.
2. Add the following to it:

```
<!DOCTYPE suite SYSTEM "http://testng.org/testng-1.0.dtd">
<suite name="Parallel Tests" verbose="1">
</suite>
```

What just happened?

We have just created our first part of TestNG file. This creates our test suite and will give us the scaffolding that is required to make our tests run in parallel later. Now that we have this in place we need to set parameters in the file that will be used to drive the tests.

Parameters in the configuration file

Now that we have created a configuration file, we need to give it some parameters that our tests can then use to start up the browser. These parameters are nodes within the `<test>` node that we are going to be adding to our `testng.xml` file. We can give our tests meaningful names so that when people have a look at the xml document they can understand what it is doing.

The `<test>` node in the TestNG configuration file also stores which test classes these parameters are going to be used in.

Let's have a look at creating a test node.

Time for action – creating a test node in the TestNG configuration

In the previous *Time for action* we created our configuration file. We now need to populate it with the test node and give it some parameters and tests that it can run against. We are going to give it the parameters for browser and the operating system as well as the hub and port that it is running on.

The classes that it can run against allow us to pass in the package that the test classes have developed. So if your organization stores all its tests classes in the `foo.bar.ui.tests` package, then you will need to pass that in the `<classes>` node.

1. Open the `TestNG` file that you created earlier.
2. Create a new `<test>` node and give it a meaningful name.
3. Create new `<parameters>` node, using the parameter node within the test node that we created. We need to give it a `name` attribute and a `value` attribute.

   When you have completed adding them they should appear as follows:

   ```
   <test name="Firefox on Windows">
     <parameter name="browser" value="firefox on windows"/>
     <classes>
       <class name="uk.co.theautomatedtester.book.Chapter10" />
     </classes>
   </test>
   ```

What just happened?

We have created our first node, which is needed to have our tests working in parallel. This is an important step and our tests will use these parameters. These parameters will be passed in where we need it so that we can start making tests in parallel. It may be worth adding more test nodes for Internet Explorer, Firefox on another Operating System, and any other browsers that you can support on your machine. Once you have finished your file should look similar to the following:

```
<! DOCTYPE suite SYSTEM "http://testng.org/testng-1.0.dtd">

<suite name="Chapter 10" verbose="1">

<test name="Firefox on Windows">
        <parameter name="browser" value="Firefox on Windows"/>
        <classes>
            <class name="uk.co.theautomatedtester.book.Chapter10" />
        </classes>
    </test>
<test name="Firefox on Linux">
        <parameter name="browser" value="Firefox on Linux"/>
        <classes>
            <class name="uk.co.theautomatedtester.book.Chapter10" />
        </classes>
</test>
```

```
<test name="IE on Windows">
        <parameter name="browser" value="IE on Windows"/>
        <classes>
            <class name="uk.co.theautomatedtester.book.Chapter10" />
        </classes>
</test>

</suite>
```

Getting our tests to use parameters

Now that we have set up our test configuration, it's time to update our tests so that we can start using TestNG and passing in the items that we need. We start by adding the `@Parameters` annotation to our test. This takes arguments which need to be that of the parameters that we created in the TestNG configuration file. We will need to update the signature of the test method to accept parameters that we can then use in our test.

Let's see this in action

Time for action – adding the parameters to our tests

Now we need to make sure that the configuration that we created for our tests actually gets into our tests and changes them accordingly. The way that we do this is by adding the `@Parameters()` annotation. We then pass in the names of the parameters that we want to use.

1. Create a new class file for testing against `http://book.theautomatedtester.co.uk/`.
2. Create a new test.
3. Add the `@Parameters` annotation to the `setUp` method.
4. Add the argument `String browser` to the signature of the `setUp` method. We are doing it against `setUp` so that we can have our tests cycling through the different browsers that are in the configuration.
5. When you have completed that, your test file should appear as follows:

```
package uk.co.theautomatedtester.book;

import com.thoughtworks.selenium.DefaultSelenium;
import com.thoughtworks.selenium.Selenium;
import org.testng.annotations.*;
```

```
public class Chapter10 {

    Selenium sel;

    @BeforeMethod(alwaysRun=true)
    @Parameters({"browser"})
    public void setUp(@Optional() String browser){
        sel =
          new DefaultSelenium(
            "192.168.157.155",
            4444,browser,
            "http://book.theautomatedtester.co.uk"
          );
        sel.start();
    }

    @Test
    public void testShouldRunATestInParallel(){
        sel.open("/");
    }

    @AfterMethod
    public void tearDown(){
        sel.stop();
    }
}
```

6. Run the test. You do this the same way that you do in JUnit and IDEA, by right-clicking on the test and then clicking on **Run item** in the context menu that loads.

What just happened?

We have successfully got a test running with TestNG. This is the first step to getting our tests running in parallel. We can see that our tests are cycling through the browser that we have placed within the configuration file.

You will have noticed that we are starting the Selenium instance with the `@BeforeMethod` and killing it with the `@AfterMethod`. This is to make sure that we have a clean Selenium instance when we are running a new test. This ensures there is no chance that a locked browser can affect a test.

However, we are still using Selenium grid as an infrastructural tool and have not managed to get our tests running in the infamous `1/n` that was mentioned at the beginning of the chapter. So how do we go about doing this?

Parallel testing

So far we have managed to get our tests cycling through different browsers by having the `<test>` node in the TestNG configuration. We have also got it working against the Selenium Grid Hub so we can see all of our tests being split out to the machines that we test against, with the varied browser and operating system combinations.

In this section we will look at how we can add a `thread-count` attribute to the `<suite>` node in our test configuration file. We also will need to add the `parallel` attribute to the test suite. The values that it takes will either be methods or classes. This will mean that either the methods and test cases are run in parallel, or the classes that contain the test cases are run in parallel.

Time for action – getting our tests running in parallel

Now that we are ready to start having our tests running in parallel, use the following steps to get started:

1. Open your `TestNG` XML configuration file.
2. Add `parallel=methods` to the suite node.
3. Add `thread-count=3` to the suite node. This will run your tests with three threads. This number can be any value that you want. It is best practice to only let this number go to the number of cores that the machine running the tests has minus the number of Selenium Remote Controls running.
4. Right-click on the configuration file in IDEA and run the tests.

What just happened?

We have just managed to get our tests running in parallel. As you can see, this has been fairly easy. We saw that adding the `parallel` and the `thread-count` attributes allows us to run these tests in parallel and when coupled with Selenium Grid we can start to get our tests running near `1/n` which is where we want our tests to be.

Pop quiz – running tests in parallel

- What is the name of the Testing Framework we used?
- Which is the main node that contains everything in the configuration file for our tests?
- What is the node inside the `<test>` node that allows us to specify the browser?
- What is the annotation we put above our `setUp()` to make sure we pass in the browser?

Have a go hero – doing more with the thing

We only tried the previous examples on two operating systems. Try expanding the examples to work on as many browser and operating system combinations as you can. Ideally, this is what your test environment will be like, so it's better to do this exercise now.

Tips and tricks for running tests in parallel

Now that we have our tests running in parallel, there are a number of things that you will notice if you have not followed the usual test automation rules. The usual items that catch people by surprise are when tests rely on each other.

Independent tests

When running tests in parallel and on Selenium Grid, keep in mind that if your tests are not independent then you will start seeing them fail for no apparent reason.

You will also need to make sure that your tests have a new browser for each test. This means that your tests always have a browser to work in, and you will not have any weird failures in your tests because of elements not being found due to a lack of a browser.

A common scenario that confuses people when it comes to parallelizing tests is what to do about registration and then logging in. The best way to handle this is to have a test that does the registration. Then have that test repeat the registration process and then log in or have a mechanism of creating an account to use at the beginning of the test.

This helps make sure that your tests keep their independence so that they easily run in parallel and follows the rule that "tests should have a known starting point".

Cleaning up tests

When writing tests for Selenium Grid that are to be run in parallel you need to make sure that your tests clean up after themselves a lot more. This is one of the key test automation rules that we learned earlier in the book, where "tests should have a known starting point".

Username and password

With our tests running in parallel, if you have an application where certain parts can only be tested by one user at a time, this is a good time to create new user accounts for each of the different aspects of your tests.

Firefox profiles

If you need to use a specific Firefox profile for your tests, you need to copy these over to the relevant machines. You will need to pass in the `-DseleniumArgs="-firefoxProfileTemplate /path/to/profile"` command when launching the Firefox Remote Control.

Summary

In this chapter we have learned how to get our tests running in parallel. We used TestNG as a way to drive our tests in a parallel fashion so that we can get our tests running as fast as possible.

Specifically, we covered topics such as:

- **Running tests in parallel**: In this section we learned how to run our tests in parallel. We also had a look at how we can cycle through different browsers using the `@Parameter` annotation.
- **Selenium tips and tricks**: In this section we learned all the tips and tricks that people may stumble across when using Selenium Grid in a parallel.

Now that we've learned about Selenium Grid and how to run tests in parallel, we have covered all that we can do with Selenium 1. We are now ready to have a look at Selenium 2, which is still in development.

11
Getting Started with Selenium 2

Now that we have learned all that we can with Selenium 1 it's now time to start having a look at what is coming up in the next version of Selenium, to be released into beta at the end of 2010. In this chapter we will be looking at the merger of the Selenium and WebDriver code bases to create what is being called Selenium 2.

We will then discuss how we can write tests using Selenium 2 to test our web applications, everything from accessing elements on the page to executing JavaScript on the page.

In this chapter we shall cover the following topics:

- Why Selenium and WebDriver are being merged
- Understanding how browser interaction will change
- Converting Selenium 1 tests to run on Selenium 2
- Starting a Selenium 2 browser instance
- Accessing elements on the page and interacting with them
- Working with JavaScript in Selenium 2

So let's get on with it...

Important preliminary points

Before starting to work through this chapter you will have to make sure that you have downloaded the latest binaries from `http://code.google.com/p/selenium/downloads/list`. You will need to download the `selenium-java-2.0*.zip` file and the `selenium-server-standalone-2.0*.jar` file. The ZIP file contains all the binaries we need for the tests and the JAR file allows us to run our tests using **RemoteWebDriver**.

Why Selenium and WebDriver are being merged

Selenium and WebDriver are being merged to create the new Selenium 2 code framework. Selenium has a very good framework for working against web applications. It has a number of positive points such as:

- Works with any browser that supports JavaScript
- More life-like interaction with the browser
- Not bound by the JavaScript sandbox
- Does not require a proxy between the test and the browser

Negative points are:

- Struggles with Same Origin Policy.
- Not all actions are equal. A Click could be a click, mouse up, or mouse down, so catering for this can be quite difficult.

WebDriver is a web-testing framework that was created by *Simon Stewart* while he was working at ThoughtWorks. It is very similar to Selenium in that it controls what the browser is doing except it does not work through JavaScript.

WebDriver works by accessing the OS and passing commands to the browser from the OS. This means that the framework is not constrained by the JavaScript Sandbox as Selenium is. We can now access items such as file inputs, so that we can test uploads and content editable DIV elements on the page. There are many more examples, but with those two updates alone we can now test items such as WYSIWYG editors.

WebDriver also does not require that you have a proxy like Selenium 1. You can use this if you want to speak to browsers on different machines, however, your test code can speak directly to the browser if they are on the same machine. This is something that is quite popular with people since it speeds up their tests a little due to there not being a "man-in-the-middle" message relay system.

The downside to WebDriver is that it requires new implementations for each of the browsers that it works against. This is due to each browser having its own access points with the Operating System.

So what if a new browser is released?

Since the Selenium community needs to release new binding code when new browsers are released, there will be some time before you can use it. This is obviously assuming that the Selenium community feel the need for this binding. While the code is being developed you will still be able to write your Selenium tests, and if there isn't a binding then Selenium will try to degrade gracefully from Selenium 2 down to Selenium 1 and use all good things Selenium.

This, and the large amount of tests already written in Selenium 1, are the main driving force behind making sure Selenium 2 is 100% backwards compatible.

How will the browser interaction change?

With Selenium Remote Control we saw the next diagram describe how we will interact with the browser. If the browser that you want to use is on the machine that you are currently on, or not, your tests will have to go through the Selenium Remote Control server.

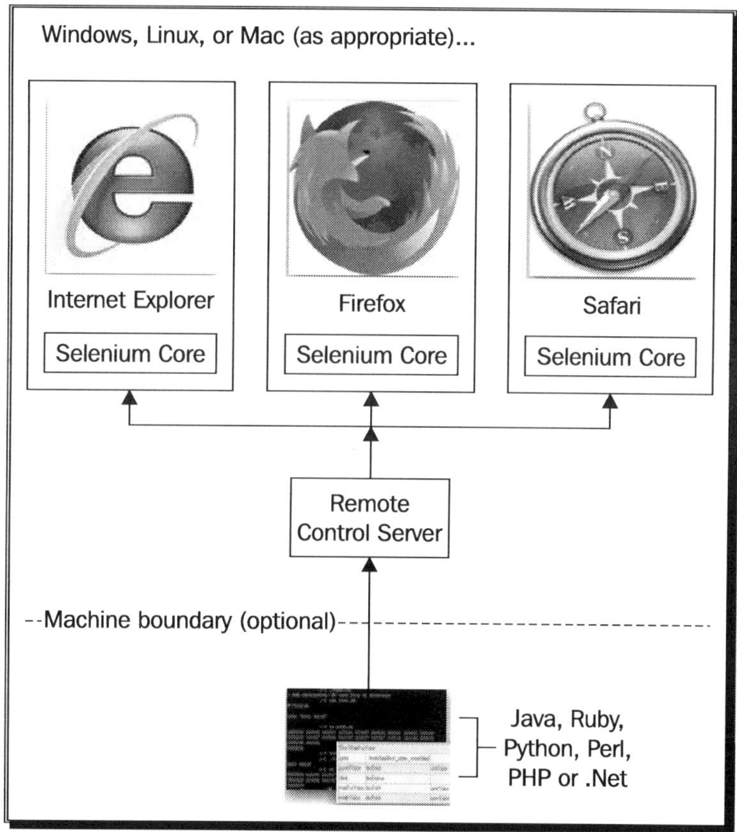

In Selenium 2 we are now making the Selenium Remote Control Server optional. This is because with Selenium 2 the Selenium Core developers are interacting with the "best fit" language for that browser. An example of this is with Firefox, we interact with the browser using JavaScript in a XPCOM object. This means that we can work on each of the different browsers without the fear of breaking its core elements. It also means that developers do not need to understand a number of different languages when developing bindings.

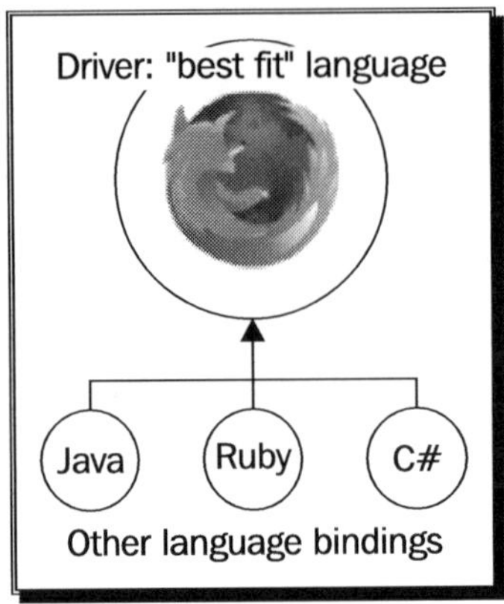

Once the bindings have been created there is a thin wrapper library created in the popular development languages. In our case we are going to see how our Java tests can interact with Firefox using the Firefox Driver that comes with Selenium 2.

If we want to test browsers that are not available on the machine that we are working on we can use the Remote WebDriver which will launch the browser that we want to test with and work with it as though it were on your machine. This has the obvious benefit of testing web applications on as many browser and operating system combinations as possible.

Now that we have a basic understanding of how our tests interact with the browser we are now ready to see how to convert our Selenium 1 tests to work with Selenium 2.

Converting Selenium 1 tests to Selenium 2

In this book we have covered all the different aspects of Selenium 1, but with Selenium 2 coming out there are now different things we can do with the browser that were not possible with Selenium 1. Unfortunately we may have spent a considerable amount of time developing Selenium 1 tests, so converting them over to the new style of Selenium 2 may not be feasible.

With this in mind the Selenium Core development team have created the `WebDriverBackedSelenium` object that we can use. This allows us to create our tests with Selenium 1 syntax that we know but have some of the benefits of WebDriver.

```
String baseUrl = "http://book.theautomatedtester.co.uk";
String remoteControl = "localhost";
Int port = 4444;
String browser = "*firefox";
Selenium selenium =
  new DefaultSelenium(remoteControl, port , browser ,baseUrl);
selenium.start()
selenium.open("/");
selenium.click("link=chapter1");
// rest of the test code
```

We then need to change our tests to the following:

```
WebDriver driver = new FirefoxDriver();
String baseUrl = "http://book.theautomatedtester.co.uk";
Selenium selenium = new WebDriverBackedSelenium(driver,baseUrl);
selenium.open("/");
selenium.click("link=chapter1");
// rest of the test code
```

Let's try converting one of our previous tests

Time for action – converting tests to Selenium 2 using WebDriverBackedSelenium

Let's take a test that we created in a previous chapter, such as the following:

```
import com.thoughtworks.selenium.*;
import org.junit.*;

public class Selenium2 {

    Selenium selenium;

    @Before
    public void setUp(){
          selenium =
             new DefaultSelenium(
               "localhost",4444,
               "*chrome","http://book.theautomatedtester.co.uk");
                   selenium.start();
```

```
    }

    @Test
    public void shouldOpenChapter2LinkAndVerifyAButton(){

    }

    @After
    public void tearDown(){
        selenium.stop();
    }
}
```

1. Open IDEA and load your example.
2. Create a new external library for the Selenium 2 binaries.
3. Add the variable WebDriver `driver` at the top of your class.
4. Change your `setUp()` to match the following snippet:

```
@Before
public void setUp(){
  driver = new FirefoxDriver();
  selenium =
    new WebDriverBackedSelenium(
      driver,
      "http://book.theautomatedtester.co.uk")
}
```

5. Change the `tearDown()` method to:

```
@After
public void tearDown(){
      driver.quit();
}
```

6. Run your tests. Your code should appear as follows:

```
@Before
public void setUp(){
  driver = new FirefoxDriver();
  selenium =
    new WebDriverBackedSelenium(
      driver, "http://book.theautomatedtester.co.uk")
}
```

```
@After
public void tearDown(){
  driver.quit();
}

@Test
Public void ShouldLoadTheSite(){
  selenium.open("/");
  selenium.clickAndWait("chapter1");
}
```

What just happened?

We have seen how with very little change to our tests we have got our old Selenium 1 tests working using the new Selenium 2 drivers. The `WebDriverBackedSelenium` object has a mapping of the Selenium 1 API to the Selenium 2 API.

When the browser starts you will see the `WebDriver` extension in the bottom right-hand side of the browser. When it is processing commands it will turn red, and when it isn't it will be black. It should look similar to the following screenshot:

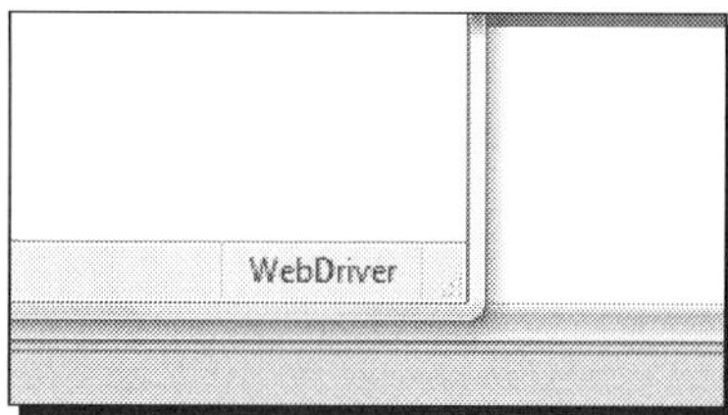

There are few items that are not fully supported by `WebDriverBackedSelenium` but hopefully as more and more work is done with the framework, these will be less noticeable.

Pop quiz

- How do you use the WebDriverBackedSelenium?

Starting a Selenium 2 browser instance

We have seen that Selenium 2 does not have to use the proxy to run its tests. It only uses the proxy to run tests that are stored on different machines that could be using different operating systems.

Starting the browser normally happens when our tests instantiate a new browser object. For example, when it executes `WebDriver driver = new FirefoxDriver();` a new browser will be executed.

There are three main browsers that are supported directly by Selenium 2. They are Google Chrome, Mozilla Firefox, and Internet Explorer. There are multiple versions of these browsers that are supported. All that your tests need to do is instantiate the browser that you want to work against and Selenium 2 will work out the rest. You do not have to use a real browser to do your testing either. The Selenium Core team have added support for HtmlUnit as a way to run your tests. To navigate to a page instead of using `open(url)` we now just need to 'get' the URL. This is because the HTTP verb `get` is slightly more intuitive.

When we have finished with the browser, all that we need to do is call the `quit()` method. This will close the browser and remove anything that it may have put on the hard drive, for example Firefox profiles and Chrome profiles. Let us have a look at what this will look like in our code.

Time for action – instantiating new browsers and closing them

In Selenium 1 we had to create a new `DefaultSelenium` object for our tests and in there pass in the browser that we want to test with. With Selenium 2 we just need to create an object for the browser that we would like to work with. The three drivers that are currently supported by Selenium are ChromeDriver for Google Chrome, FirefoxDriver for Mozilla Firefox and InternetExplorerDriver for Internet Explorer.

1. Create a new project in IDEA and reference the Selenium 2 binaries.
2. Create a new Selenium test class.
3. Create the variable `WebDriver` driver; at the top of our class.
4. In the `setUp()` method put `driver = new FirefoxDriver()`. This will start up a Mozilla Firefox instance.
5. In the `tearDown()` method put `driver.quit()`. This will close the browser and clean up anything that it did when starting the browser.
6. Create an empty test and run it. You should see a browser open, as seen in the following screenshot:

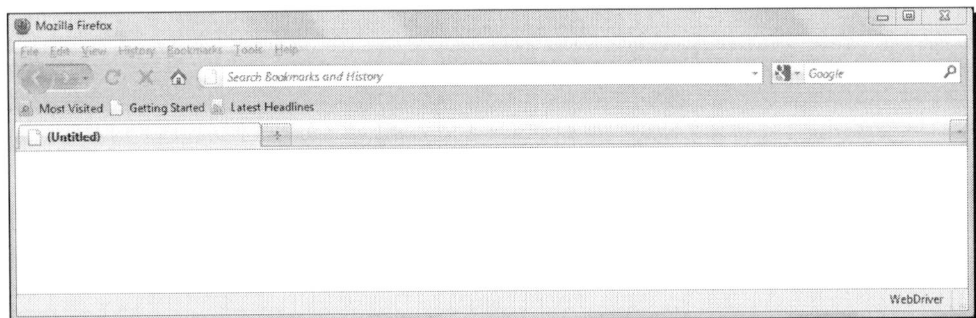

What just happened?

We have successfully created a new browser instance and launched the browser so that we can start running our tests against it. When we have finished with the browser we can then call the `quit()` method which will close the browser then clean up anything that may have been created when Selenium 2 was trying the launch the browser.

Pop quiz

- How do we start a browser for our tests to use?

Have a go hero

Now that you have successfully launched a Mozilla Firefox instance, try and do the same with Google Chrome and Internet Explorer.

Accessing elements on the page and interacting with them

The way that our tests interact with elements on the page has changed quite dramatically from Selenium 1. In Selenium 1 you would make an API call passing in a locator and any extra information that is needed. For example, to type you would use:

```
selenium.typeKeys("id=inputField","Selenium is cool");
```

This meant that the readability of the tests was quite poor since you needed to check all the parameters of the API call.

Selenium 2 has changed this. In your tests you now have an object that maps directly to the element on the page from where you can use it. We are able to map elements by telling our browser object to find the element we want and to give us a new Selenium 2 `WebElement` object. The `findElement()` method takes one parameter which tells the driver how to find the object.

This is stored in the static class **By**. `By` has a number of different methods as we can see in the following list:

- By.id("idOfObject")
- By.linkText("TextUsedInTheLink")
- By.partialLinkText("partOfThelink")
- By.tagName("theHTMLNodeType")
- By.className("cssClassOnTheElement")

- By.cssSelector("cssSelectorToTheElement")
- By.xpath("//Xpath/to/the/element")
- By.name("nameOfElement")

An example of the code is given next:

```
@Test
public void shouldLoadTheSiteAndClickChapter1(){
        driver.get("http://book.theautoamtedtester.co.uk");
        WebElement link =
          driver.findElement(By.linkText("somelink"));
        link.click();
    }
```

The `WebElement` that is returned is immutable. This means that the element cannot be changed once it has been created. This has been done so that Selenium 2 can be as life-like as possible and end-users will not be able to change things as they want.

Let's now see this in action...

Time for action – finding a link and clicking it

Imagine that you want to test clicking on the links on the page. To do this we will need to make a WebElement for the link that we want to click and then click on it. Our example is going to click on the `Chapter1` link and then close the browser.

1. Create a new Java class.
2. Create a test that will open `http://book.theautomatedtester.co.uk`.
3. Click the link `Chapter1`.
4. Close the browser.
5. Run your tests. The code for your tests should appear similar to the following:

```
@Test
public void shouldLoadTheSiteAndClickChapter1(){
    driver.get("http://book.theautoamtedtester.co.uk");
    WebElement inputField =
      driver.findElement(By.linkText("Chapter1"));
    inputField.click();
}
```

What just happened?

We have successfully created a Selenium 2 test that loads an URL and then clicks on a link that has the text `Chapter1`. Our test showed how the driver finds the elements and returns a `WebElement` that is mapped to an element on the page. We can then interact with it as we want, as long as the element supports that type of interaction.

Finding elements with XPath

In Selenium 1 we saw how we can use XPath in our tests to find elements that are on the page and that do not fit any of the different locator strategies. Selenium 2 allows this locator strategy as well. We do this by calling `By.xpath` and passing in `xpath` as a parameter.

Time for action – finding an element with XPath

Imagine that you need to interact with an element on the page but do not know the ID or the name of the element. In Chapter 2, *Locators*, we saw a number of different XPath strategies so let us try to translate our test cases into Selenium 2.

1. Create a new Java class and create the `setUp()` and `tearDown()` methods.
2. The test needs to load `http://book.theautomatedtester.co.uk/chapter2`.
3. Find the element with the text **Sibling Button**.
4. Click on the button.
5. Run your test. Your code should appear as follows:

```
@Test
public void shouldLoadChapter2AndClickOnSiblingButton(){
  driver.get("http://book.theautomatedtester.co.uk");
  WebElement sibling =
    driver.FindElement(
      By.xpath("//input[@value='Button with ID']
      /following-sibling::input[@value='Sibling Button']"
      )
  );
  Sibling.click();
}
```

What just happened?

We have just seen how our tests can use `xpath` to find elements on the page so that our tests can use them. There is no difference between Selenium 1 and Selenium 2 when it comes to finding elements by XPath.

One thing to note is that XPath in Selenium 2 is still slow. This is due to the nature of the DOM. It is still recommended that you follow the same locator best practises that have been discussed in this book.

Finding multiple elements

There are times where we will want to find all elements that match some criteria. For example if we need to find all the divs on the page with the `xpath //div` but we use `findElement` it will return the first element that matches the `xpath` and then our tests will continue. There are times where there are a number of elements that match that criteria and will want to interact with each of them or even one of them that is not the first element.

To do this we need to use the `findElements` method. This, similar to the `findElement` method, takes one parameter which is the `By` object to tell the driver how to find the object. The driver will then return a list of all the WebElements that match our search. The list that is returned is immutable so you will not be able to add or remove items in the list.

We can then access the list to get the element that we want to work with. We can see an example in the following snippet:

```
List<WebElement> myList =
  driver.findElements(By.xpath("//some/Xpath"));
        myList.get(1).click();
```

Let's see this in action now...

Time for action – finding multiple elements on the page

Imagine that your test requires you to type something into each of the input boxes on the page, or if you needed to check how many buttons were on the page.

In this scenario, the `findElements` method call will be extremely useful and we can tell the driver to search by `tagName` to find all of the items on the page.

1. Create a new test to access `http://book.theautomatedtester.co.uk/chapter2`.
2. Find all elements that are an input.
3. Assert whether the list size is five.

4. Run your test. It should appear as follows:

```
@Test
public void shouldLoadChapter2AndFindAllInputElements(){
    driver.get("http://book.theautoamtedtester.co.uk");
    List<WebElement> inputs =
      driver.findElements(By.tagName("input"));
    Assert.assertEquals("Should be 5",5,inputs.size());
}
```

What just happened?

We have just looked at the `findElements` method. This can be used when there are multiple elements on the page that match the search criteria. This could be because there are a number of items that match our XPath but we do not want to work with the first element that matches on the page, or if we just want to get all the input elements on a form to be able to type into them.

Typing into input fields

Filling in forms is one of the most common uses for Selenium. To do this we need to get a `WebElement` object and then call the `sendKeys` method. The parameter it takes is a string of what we want to type. Selenium will then send a message to the operating system to put it into the text box. This is one of the method calls that demonstrates major differences between Selenium 1 and Selenium 2.

Time for action – typing into a text box

Imagine that you need to type something into a text box. To do this we need to get an element and then use the `sendKeys` method.

1. Create a new test case.
2. Navigate to `http://book.theautomatedtester.co.uk/chapter1`.
3. Type into the textbox `storeinput`.
4. Run your test. Its code should appear as follows:

```
@Test
public void shouldTypeIntoATextBox(){
    driver.get("http://www.theautomatedtester.co.uk/chapter1");
    WebElement textBox = driver.findElement(By.id("storeinput"));
    textBox.sendKeys("I can type");
}
```

What just happened?

We have successfully typed into a text box. The `sendKeys` method sends the string we want to appear in the element. We can also send through keys that users are likely to use, such as *Return*. To send through these keys there is the static object called `Keys`. To press *Return* your test would have something like `textbox.sendKeys(Keys.Return)`. This is a better implementation than in Selenium 1 where we needed to know the ASCII code for the key that we wanted to press.

Real-life interaction

Selenium 2 will try to mimic what real users can do as closely as possible. One of the main complaints about Selenium was the way that a test could click on a link that was hidden or type into a textbox that was not visible. While there may be times when this will be useful, for the most part it isn't. Let's see how this wouldn't work.

Time for action – working with hidden elements throws errors

In this case we are going to make sure that the element that we want to work with is not allowed.

1. Create a new test.
2. Navigate to `http://book.theautomatedtester.co.uk/chapter1`.
3. Find the input box with `hiddenTextBox` as the ID. It is not visible.
4. Get Selenium 2 to type into it.
5. Run your test. Its code should appear as follows:

```
@Test
public void shouldNotBeAbleToInteractWithElement(){
    driver.get("http://www.theautomatedtester.co.uk/chapter1");
    WebElement textBox =
        driver.findElement(By.id("hiddenTextBox "));
    textBox.sendKeys("I should throw an error");
}
```

6. When it has completed, your test should have failed.

What just happened?

We have seen how Selenium tries to interact with the application under test just as an end user would. This allows our tests to gain more value in that they truly are doing the same as a user.

Since things are a lot more life-like you will also be able to try it on content editable elements in the page. This is something that Selenium 1 could not do because it was synthesizing interaction on the page with JavaScript.

Speaking of JavaScript, let us have a look at how running JavaScript from our tests has changed after we have completed the next *Pop quiz*.

Pop quiz

- How do Selenium 1 and Selenium 2 differ in the way that they manage elements on the page?
- What happens when you find a hidden element and work with it?

Have a go hero

Try working with different types of elements on the page and see how well you fare. Try working with Selects and Content editable areas. It will also be very good to try and create tests that wait for elements to appear on that page.

Working with JavaScript in Selenium 2

In previous chapters we saw how to use JavaScript to do what we want in our tests. We saw how we can use it to create unique items or to access items on the page. In Selenium 1 we had to access the page through the Selenium `browserbot` object that is injected to the page. This is the object that controls the page for our tests.

Since Selenium 2 is working with the browser in a more native fashion we can just pass in the JavaScript that we want to use on the page. We do this by casting the driver to a `JavaScriptExecutor` object and then calling the `executeScript` method with the script that we want it to run.

Let's see this in action...

Time for action – using JavaScript in Selenium 2

Imagine that you want to check that a select has a certain amount of options. In Selenium 1 we used the `Chapter4` page in our test. We used the JavaScript `this.browserbot.getUserWindow().document.getElementById("selecttype").options.length` to get the amount of options in the select. This is quite a bit of JavaScript that is needed. In Selenium 2 all we need to do is write `document.getElementById("selecttype").options.length`. This is more readable for anyone who has not used Selenium therefore making the learning curve shallower to the new users of the framework.

Let's create a test that checks the value is `4`.

1. Create a new test.
2. Navigate to `http://book.theautomatedtester.co.uk/chapter4`.
3. Verify that `selecttype` only has four options in it.
4. Run your test. The test code should appear similar to the following:

```
@Test
public void shouldExecuteJavaScript(){
    driver.get("http://book.theautomatedtester.co.uk/chapter4");
    Assert.assertTrue((Boolean)
            ((JavascriptExecutor)driver)
                .executeScript(
                  "return document.getElementById('selecttype')
                  .options.length === 4"
                )
    );
}
```

What just happened?

We have successfully run some JavaScript against the page using what is considered common JavaScript. The script just finds the element on the page and then works with it. To execute the script we need to cast the driver object to a `JavascriptExecutor` object.

Returning something from your JavaScript to your test

If we are executing some JavaScript that is going to return anything Selenium will return a generic object. We can then cast this object to what we expect it to be. In the example above we saw how it could be cast to a Boolean so that we can use it. This is because Selenium will try to return a POJO to your test. A **POJO** is a **Plain Old Java Object** which allows casting to different types to happen without much effort. Let's see how we can use this in our tests.

Time for action – returning from executing JavaScript

In this example we are going to try and return a dictionary that will hold some information that is being stored on the page. In our example we are going to return a dictionary that will hold a button ID, and the button's value that is visible to the user.

1. Create a new test case.
2. Navigate to `http://book.theautomatedtester.co.uk/chapter4`.

3. Find all elements with the tag `input` using JavaScript. The code will be:

```
var inputs = document.getElementsByTag("input");
```

4. Iterate through the results of the call putting the ID of the button as the key and the value of the button as its target.

5. Return the dictionary that has been created.

6. Run your tests. It should look similar to the following snippet:

```
@Test
public void shouldExecuteJavaScriptAndReturnADictionary(){
    driver.get("http://book.theautomatedtester.co.uk/chapter4");
    Dictionary<String, Object> myDict
      = (Dictionary<String, Object>)
            ((JavascriptExecutor)driver)
                   .executeScript("var inputs
                     = document.getElementsByTag('input')," +
                          "myDict = {};" +
                          "for (i = 0;i<inputs.length;i++)
                            {" +
                             " myDict[inputs[i].id]
                               = inputs[i].value;" +
                            "}" +
                            "return myDict;");
}
```

What just happened?

In this section we have returned a dictionary that we can use in our tests. This is quite useful if you want to get a number of different items off the page and you only want to make one JavaScript call.

We can do this with all different base types. In the previous example, we saw how it returned a Boolean so all that we needed to do was cast the object and then do an Assert.

Pop quiz

- Are you still required to use `browserbot` in your JavaScript?
- To run the JavaScript, what do you need to do?
- Can your JavaScript return to your test?
- What does it return?

Have a go hero

Try creating more tests with Selenium 2 so that they return different data types that your tests will need to cast to. This will give you a better appreciation of what Selenium 2 JavaScript can and can't do.

Summary

We learned a lot in this chapter about the upcoming release of Selenium 2. There has been a lot of work to merge the WebDriver and Selenium code bases to try to make the best web testing framework.

Specifically, we covered the following topics:

- **Why Selenium and WebDriver are being merged**: Both Selenium and WebDriver have their pros and cons. Fortunately, their pros cancel out the other's cons so that we can now get a lot more web applications tested. We also saw how Selenium 2 is 100% backwards-compatible with Selenium 1 so that prior work by testers and developers will not be wasted.
- **How will the browser interaction change?** Selenium 2 allows us to create tests that do not need to go through a proxy. We saw how our tests speak to the browser using the "best fit" language API to that browser without having to understand how it works.
- **Converting Selenium 1 tests to Selenium 2**: Selenium 1 tests will be around for a very long time, hence having a way to migrate tests with the least amount of effort was created. This is the `WebDriverBackedSelenium` object that means changing your tests will only be two changes in your Java classes. This change is creating a `WebDriver` object in your test and then injecting it to your `WebDriverBackedSelenium`.
- **Starting a new browser instance**: Since Selenium 2 does not rely on the proxy in the middle to start up browser instances, instantiating new `Browser` objects will startup the browser up. Once done we can then close the browser by calling the `quit()` method.
- **Accessing elements on the page and interacting with them**: We saw how interacting with elements on the page has changed so much between Selenium 1 and Selenium 2. In Selenium 1 we had to pass in the locator for the element in the API call, whereas in Selenium 2 we can now map elements on the page to immutable objects in our tests using the `WebElement` object. This object then controls how we can access and throw errors if we try to do something that element cannot handle. For example toggling a Select box as if it were a checkbox. We also had a look at how we can find multiple objects that meet the search criteria that we had created with the `By` object. Finally, in this section, we had a look at how we can type into elements that can be typed into.

- **Working with JavaScript in Selenium 2**: In this section we saw how using JavaScript has become a lot easier to do since we do not need to access browserbot anymore. Our scripts just need to be able to do what they normally would if it were running on the page. We also had a look at how returning something from the JavaScript that we want to run is converted to the data type that is native to the language we are creating our tests in.

Selenium 2 is still in development, but it is starting to become very stable. The only changes that are expected in the near future are enhancements. These enhancements will hopefully help it handle more HTML 5 elements.

Pop Quiz Answers

Chapter 1 – Getting Started with Selenium IDE

- What is the main language that drives Selenium IDE?
    - **Answer**: JavaScript
- Selenium IDE works on Internet Explorer?
    - **Answer**: False
- Selenium verifies items on the page when it is recording steps?
    - **Answer**: False
- What is the difference between verify and assert?
    - **Answer**: A verify command validates and verifies that an element is on the page but does not interrupt the execution of the test. Assert is similar to a verify command except that it will cause the test to fail and interrupt its execution.
- If you wanted to validate that a button has appeared is on a page which two commands would be the best to use?
    - **Answer**: verifyElementPresent/assertElementPresent
- If an element got added after the page has loaded what command would you use to make sure the test passed in the future?
    - **Answer**: `waitForElementPresent`
- How do we run all the tests in a Test Suite?
    - **Answer**: Click on the button with the Arrow and three solid green lines

Chapter 2 – Locators

- What color is an element bordered with when the Find button is clicked in Selenium IDE?
    - Answer: Green
- If you wanted to use JavaScript to find the element on the page, which strategy would you use to find it?
    - Answer: DOM locator strategy
- Pick two from below if you wanted do a partial match on an attribute on an element from the beginning of the value
    - Answer: `contains()` and `starts-with`
- What is the most common way to find an element on a page?
    - Answer: ID
- If you wanted to find the sibling input that is after an input in the DOM, what would the XPath look like?
    - Answer: `//input/following-sibling::input`
- What would the CSS look like for the above question?
    - Answer: `css=input + input`

Chapter 3 – Pattern Matching

- `Does exact:` allows capitalization differences?
    - **Answer**: False
- Does `exact:` only work on text in links?
    - **Answer**: No, it can be used on any elements that have test
- What will the `* item` in a glob pattern do for `goog*`?
    - **Answer**: It will do a wildcard match to find anything that has 'goog' as its first four letters.
- What will the `?` item do in the glob patter `?ool` ?
    - **Answer**: It will match any words that are four characters long and the last three letters are 'ool'

- What is the best way to check if a word is three characters long?
  - **Answer**: `\w{3}`
- What is the way to add wild cards to a regular expression?
  - **Answer**: Use the `.` in the regular expression

Chapter 4 – Using JavaScript

- What is the syntax to use JavaScript in a test?
  - **Answer**: `javascript{ 1 + 1 }`
- In a multiline JavaScript Statement how do you return to Selenium?
  - **Answer**: The last line in a multiline statement will return if it is not a statement that moves the result into a variable. For example `b = 1 + 1` will not return but `1 + 1` will.
- What is the variable that stores all the Selenium variables?
  - Answer: storedVars
- What is the object that allows our tests to access the page?
  - Answer: browserbot
- Does waitForCondition sit inside or outside the selenium object?
  - Answer: Its inside the selenium object

Chapter 5 – User Extensions and Add-ons

- How do you store variables to be used later in the test?
  - **Answer**: Use the `storedVars` dictionary
- Can your user extension call other commands such as `type` and `click` ?
  - **Answer**: Yes, they can. The commands need to call the do function name like `doType` or do click so that it can be used.
- Can your user extension access the DOM programmatically?
  - **Answer**: Yes it can. The extension can access the DOM and other JavaScript APIs in the format that we saw in the previous chapter. This means that we can create new commands just for the API, making tests more verbose and easier to read.

- How can a new command, created in an extension, fail a test if the new command is doing a verify?
    - **Answer**: The command will have to create a new `CommandComplete` object setting the property `failed` to either true or false. It is good practice to have a message in the object if the step does fail so that it can be outputted to the screen. Once the object has been populated it is passed as an argument to the `commandComplete` method.
- What is a Selenium IDE add-on?
    - **Answer**: The Selenium IDE Add-on is a Mozilla Firefox add-on that allows you to extend Selenium beyond what a User-Extension can do. This then attaches itself Selenium IDE so that you can use it in conjunction with Selenium.

Chapter 6 – First Steps with Selenium RC

- Where can you download Selenium Remote Control?
    - **Answer**: All of the Selenium tools are available from `http://seleniumhq.org/download`.
- When you have placed Selenium Remote Control somewhere accessible how do you start Selenium Remote Control?
    - **Answer**: Open up a Command Prompt or a terminal window and navigate to where you have placed Selenium Remote Control. Type the command `java -jar selenium-server-standalone.jar`.
- Are you allowed to use relative paths to the Test Suite and results file
    - **Answer**: False
- What is the argument needed to make your tests run within Firefox?
    - **Answer**: `*firefox`
- What is the argument needed to make your tests run within Internet Explorer?
    - **Answer**: `*iexplore`
- What is the argument that allows our tests to use User Extensions with our tests?
    - **Answer**: `-userExtension c:\path\to\UserExtension.js`

Chapter 7 – Creating Selenium Remote Control Tests

- Do you need to create a folder for your tests?
  - **Answer**: Yes. This will tell your IDE that you will keep test code in here. It will also make sure that we have separated concerns. This will allow us to create our web applications and keep our tests close by.
- How does one export their Selenium IDE tests into a programming language?
  - **Answer**: From within Selenium IDE you go **File | Export Tests As ...** and then chose from one of the different languages that is supported there.
- Do you need to have Selenium JAR files as a dependency of your tests?
  - **Answer**: Yes. Selenium Remote Control works by having a client-server interface with Selenium Server accepting commands from your tests
- How do you run your tests once the dependencies are correct?
  - **Answer**: It is a simple case of right-clicking and then clicking on **Run Test**. You could use the shortcut of *Ctrl* + *Shift* + *F10*.
- How many parameters does the Selenium object take when using `DefaultSelenium`?
  - **Answer**: 4
- What class do we need to extend when writing JUnit 3 style tests?
  - **Answer**: `SeleneseTestCase`
- If we are running Selenium Server, can we use a different `setUp()` method?
  - **Answer**: If we call `setUp()` and pass in two parameters, the browser string and site URL, or if we pass in the `siteURL` it will make assumptions like the Selenium Server is on the same machine.
- How do you start the browser?
  - **Answer**: Call the `start()` function
- How do you stop the browser?
  - **Answer**: Call the `stop()` function

- How do I do asserts and verifies in when writing tests in a programming language?
    - **Answer**: Verifies and asserts are done using the testing framework's asserts. If you want to do a Selenium Assert on a Element on the page it would be `assertTrue(selenium.isElementPresent ("elementLocator");`. If you wanted do a Selenium Verify you would wrap the assert in a `try{ } catch{ }` block so that it can carry on even if the assert fails.
- What is the Page Object design pattern?
    - **Answer**: The Page Object pattern gives us a way to abstract our tests away so that we can make these tests more maintainable. We can make tests that only require updating if new steps have been added otherwise it just requires the page object to be updated.

Chapter 8 – Advanced Selenium Techniques

- How would you get a cookie by name?
    - **Answer**: `getCookieByName(string)` will return a string that has the value of the cookie.
- How would you get all the cookies that are on the page?
    - **Answer**: `getCookie()` will return all the items on the page
- What is returned from `getCookie`?
    - **Answer**: A string that contains all the cookies. It is delimited by a semicolon so the string can be split on that into an array which can be iterated over for the assertions.
- What is the default file type for capturing screenshots?
    - **Answer**: PNG
- How does one capture a screenshot of the entire desktop?
    - **Answer**: Call `captureScreenshot("/path/to/file.png")`
- When capturing shots to string, how is the string encoded?
    - **Answer**: The strings that are returned are in `Base64`
- What is the name of the library we used to record video?
    - **Answer**: Castro

- What is the desktop viewing application Castro relies on?
    - **Answer**: VNC

Chapter 9 – Getting Started with Selenium Grid

- What is the command required to start the Hub?
    - **Answer:** `ant launch-hub`
- What is the URL where one can see what is happening on the grid?
    - **Answer:** `http://nameofmachine:4444/console` where `nameofmachine` is the name of the machine that is running the hub. If it is on the same machine as you are currently on, use `localhost` or `127.0.0.1`.
- How do you specify the port the Remote Control is running on?
    - **Answer**:`-Dport=portNumber`
- How do you specify which browser you would like the remote control to be registered with?
    - **Answer**: `-Denvironment=target` where `target` is the target or name from the grid configuration.

Chapter 10 – Running Selenium Tests in Parallel

- What is the name of the Testing Framework we used?
    - **Answer**: TestNG
- What is the main node that contains everything in the configuration file for our tests?
    - **Answer**: Suite
- What is the node inside the `<test>` node that allows us to specify the browser?
    - **Answer**: Parameter
- What is the annotation we put above our `setUp()` to make sure we pass in the browser?
    - **Answer**: `@Parameter({"parameterName"})`

Chapter 11 – Getting started with Selenium 2

- How do you use the `WebDriverBackedSelenium`?
    - **Answer**: Create a new instance of the browser you want to use using Selenium 2. Then pass this into the `WebDriverBackedSelenium` with the URL that you would like to test. It will look like this:

    ```
    @Before
    public void setUp(){
        driver = new FirefoxDriver();
        selenium =
          new WebDriverBackedSelenium(driver, http://book.
    theautomatedtester.co.uk)
    }
    ```

- How do we start a browser for our tests to use?
    - **Answer**. We just need to instantiate it before our tests are expecting to use it, for example `driver = new FirefoxDriver()`
- How does Selenium 1 and Selenium 2 differ in the way that it manages elements on the page?
    - **Answer**: In Selenium 1 we had to pass in the locator to an element in the API call. In Selenium 2 we need to find the element on the page with Selenium 2 and then interact with it
- What happens when you find a hidden element and work with it?
    - **Answer**: Selenium 2 works very hard at trying to imitate what the user is likely to do. Selenium will find the hidden element but it will throw exceptions if you try to type or click on it
- Are you still required to use Browserbot in your JavaScript?
    - **Answer**: No
- To run the JavaScript, what do you need to do?
    - **Answer**: The code in the test needs to cast the driver to a `JavascriptExecutor` object and then call the `execute` method passing in the JavaScript snippet we would like it to execute
- Can your JavaScript return to your test?
    - **Answer**: Yes
- What does it return?
    - **Answer**: It returns a Plain Old Java Object (POJO) so that we can then cast it to the type that we need within our tests

Index

G

H

I

J

K

L

T

U

V

W

X

Thank you for buying
Selenium 1.0 Testing Tools Beginner's Guide

About Packt Publishing

Packt, pronounced 'packed', published its first book "*Mastering phpMyAdmin for Effective MySQL Management*" in April 2004 and subsequently continued to specialize in publishing highly focused books on specific technologies and solutions.

Our books and publications share the experiences of your fellow IT professionals in adapting and customizing today's systems, applications, and frameworks. Our solution based books give you the knowledge and power to customize the software and technologies you're using to get the job done. Packt books are more specific and less general than the IT books you have seen in the past. Our unique business model allows us to bring you more focused information, giving you more of what you need to know, and less of what you don't.

Packt is a modern, yet unique publishing company, which focuses on producing quality, cutting-edge books for communities of developers, administrators, and newbies alike. For more information, please visit our website: `www.packtpub.com`.

About Packt Open Source

In 2010, Packt launched two new brands, Packt Open Source and Packt Enterprise, in order to continue its focus on specialization. This book is part of the Packt Open Source brand, home to books published on software built around Open Source licences, and offering information to anybody from advanced developers to budding web designers. The Open Source brand also runs Packt's Open Source Royalty Scheme, by which Packt gives a royalty to each Open Source project about whose software a book is sold.

Writing for Packt

We welcome all inquiries from people who are interested in authoring. Book proposals should be sent to author@packtpub.com. If your book idea is still at an early stage and you would like to discuss it first before writing a formal book proposal, contact us; one of our commissioning editors will get in touch with you.

We're not just looking for published authors; if you have strong technical skills but no writing experience, our experienced editors can help you develop a writing career, or simply get some additional reward for your expertise.

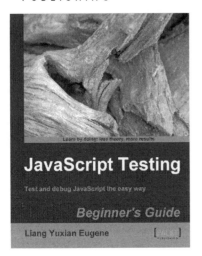

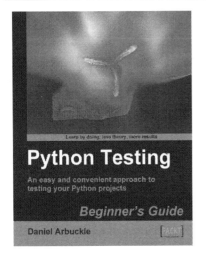

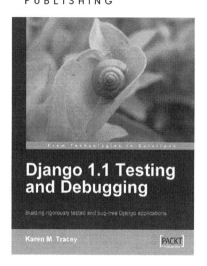

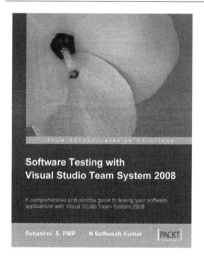

Made in the USA
Lexington, KY
27 July 2011